THE ARTHURS, NELSONS AND SCHOOLS
OF THE SOUTHERN

The Arthurs, Nelsons and Schools of the Southern

S. C. TOWNROE

LONDON

IAN ALLAN

First published 1973

ISBN 0 7110 0434 X

Published by Ian Allan Ltd, Shepperton, Surrey and printed in the
United Kingdom by A. Wheaton & Co, Exeter

Contents

Introduction to the Original Editions

The Southern Railway's King Arthur class of seventy-four 4-6-0 express passenger locomotives became one of the most popular types in the country during the years of the grouped railways. They were to be seen everywhere, from Ramsgate to Exeter, from Oxford to Brighton. Whether you took your summer holiday on the Continent or in Devonshire it was almost certain that the journey by rail would be behind a King Arthur at some stage, an engine with a workman-like appearance and a legendary name.

To locomotive enthusiasts, for whom this book is written, they were more than just a class, for there were to be four precise groups or batches of engines varying in detail one from the other and representing the growth of a design over a period of years. The story of their growth is interesting from the technical point of view, and now that these fine engines are no longer masters of the primary express traffic on the Southern Region, their story is one that should be told.

The King Arthur class had not long been named when another more powerful 4-6-0, the Lord Nelson, appeared on the scene. Sixteen engines of the Nelson class were not, however, likely to do more than take a little of the cream of the express traffic away from the seventy-four Arthurs, and, in fact, they only succeeded in taking away a few star turns, mainly in the way of Pullman expresses. Even then, Arthurs were often to be seen working in place of Nelsons, and the whisper went round amateur railway circles that the Nelsons were just white elephants. The lack of really definite evidence to that effect merely stimulated such rumours. "Confidentially, old man," one amateur might say to another, " 'X' told me that they are always under repair"; or, "It was a rotten run—the driver told me at Victoria that the Nelsons won't steam." Partisans of the Arthurs were not slow to add first to the fire of contention, naturally. "The Nelsons had to hand it to the Arthurs west of Salisbury, you know". Nelson supporters replied by quoting a comment which a leading locomotive engineer was alleged to have made after a footplate trip on an Arthur, to the effect that it was a "crude engine".

Heated discussions between the champions of different designs will no doubt continue until standardisation on British Railways has eliminated all comparisons, by producing one type of engine for each class of traffic, if ever it succeeds in doing so.

The most powerful 4-4-0 in Europe! This distinction was claimed for a new design of 4-4-0 introduced by the Southern Railway in 1930, and wide interest was aroused in railway circles at the revival of the four-coupled type for main-line work, in view of the general preference for six-coupled types.

There were certain loading gauge restrictions over the London–Hastings route to be met by the design. It was hardly anticipated that the new engines would prove to have such a wide usefulness over all the Southern main-lines, or that they would, in the course of their career, run the six-coupled engines so close in performance.

Superlatives have often been used in describing new locomotives, and descriptions of that kind can be as meaningless as the grandiloquent claims made by US film companies for each new production of their studios. It has been wisely said that the true worth of any design must be judged by long-term results. The long view must be taken because, amongst other things, the repair and maintenance expenses and the fuel consumption can only be truly assessed after a period of years in traffic. If the design is to be considered for a place amongst the *élite*, the performance and reliability of the engines must be maintained when they are no longer new, when they are matched against other and possibly newer designs, and when, under changing traffic conditions, they are given loads to handle in excess of those for which they were intended. On this basis, a just assessment of the Schools class engines and their work must be that their designer produced an outstanding class of locomotive.

The fact that amongst the enginemen in particular the popularity of these engines has never waned is a tribute in itself. Whatever the odds, they display on the road a response to handling and a degree of stamina which find favour with the practical man on the footplate.

Like all engines, they bear an official classification, namely 'V' class. Some types become known merely by letters, as B's or X's, while others acquire nicknames, not always complimentary; the Schools have always been spoken of as such. "Give me a School any day, with a fair load" is a remark often heard from experienced drivers. It seems unlikely that any more large 4-4-0s will ever be built by British Railways. In that case, the Schools class will pass into locomotive history as the last and the best of them.

1947–49   S. C. TOWNROE

Preface

'Of the making of railway books there is no end.'

These words might be an apt comment upon the number of books published in the last decade, although they are quoted from a book published as long ago as 1928 by that doyen of railway authors, Cecil J. Allen.* It is virtually impossible nowadays to write a new railway book that entirely avoids any repetition of information previously published; without it, on the other hand, the narrative would be disjointed. The theme of this volume was originally written by the author in two booklets published by Ian Allan, entitled *The Book of the Schools Class* (1947) and *King Arthurs and Lord Nelsons of the SR* (1949). A critic of the latter was kind enough to recommend it as 'a good, potted account'. As the booklets are long out of print, the publishers asked me to rewrite them in a combined, and less potted, version. In doing so, the author has endeavoured to set the story within the contemporary scene, and to include some recollections of the Southern Railway and Region, when he was one of the locomotive engineers.

In the search for old records, a file with the numbers of locomotives allocated to the various sheds in 1937 turned up in a drawer in the Waterloo offices, but official papers pre-1940 were cleared out in a wartime salvage drive, and later were thrown away at the end of steam traction. In sifting through old photographs from various sources, a surprising number were found to be undated. Such are some of the difficulties that confront an historian of even so comparatively recent a period of railway history, in striving for accuracy.

In compiling the original booklets the author was indebted to H. Holcroft, who was responsible for much of the design work on Maunsell's locomotives, and who later published his own memoirs. Acknowledgement is due to former members of the Southern Railway, including L. Lynes (Maunsell's Carriage & Wagon Assistant), M. S. Hatchell (Works Manager), the late A. Earle Edwards (Traffic Superintendent), the late J. P. Maitland (Shed Superintendent, Nine Elms), S. A. Downes (District Locomotive Superintendent). Train Running records were contributed by Cecil J. Allen and

Railway Planning & Making, Cecil J. Allen. Longmans, Green & Co (1928).

9

John G. Webber. Thanks are due to the photographers and to the donor of prints from pre-Group official negatives which are privately preserved.

A bibliography is included of publications found useful in writing this book.

Finally, this book must be dedicated to the memory of men whose lives were bound up with the steam locomotive, and whose cheerful good humour may perhaps be faintly detected in these pages.

Shawford, Hampshire   S. C. TOWNROE

The Southern and its First Chief Mechanical Engineer

At the time of the amalgamation of the railways in Britain into four group companies in 1923, the railways south of the Thames which were to form the new Southern Railway did not enjoy much of a reputation for speed, comfort and punctuality. In the public esteem they were not in the same street as the Great Western—which could probably have claimed the largest band of devotees—or the London & North Western or Great Northern. By 1939, the Southern had become known as 'Britain's brightest and best-run line', an image of which the foremost ingredients were the regularity and frequency of its electrified services, the geniality of its staff as portrayed by that poster character, 'Sunny South Sam', and by the comfort and punctuality of its main-line steam trains. The latter were to be associated with its three principal types of express locomotives, the King Arthurs, the Schools and the Lord Nelsons, which are the theme of this book.

Of those 140 locomotives, five have survived for preservation. King Arthur class No 777 *Sir Lamiel*, Schools class No 925 *Cheltenham* and No 850 *Lord Nelson* were withheld from scrapping by the British Railways Board, and at the time of writing have as yet no permanent homes. Schools class No 926 *Repton* was sold to a purchaser in the USA and No 928 *Stowe* was acquired by Lord Montagu for his museum at Beaulieu.

Four years elapsed between the Armistice of 1918 and the creation of the Southern Railway, and of the GWR, LNER and LMS, in 1923; four years of uncertainty for railway management, years in which forward planning for the rehabilitation of the war-worn railways in the South was inhibited. The Government, indeed, retained the control of the railways, which had begun at the outbreak of war, until 1921: meantime those railway politicians who had from time to time argued in favour of nationalisation aired their views more vehemently. The Ministry of Transport, in 1920, proposed in a White Paper the fusion of the private companies into six groups to be known as the Western, North-Western, Eastern, North-Eastern

Scottish and London groups. In due course a counter-proposal came from the Railway Companies Association for five groups; four were the ones eventually adopted in 1923, the fifth was to have been a 'London group' to co-ordinate the special transport problems of the Metropolis, an idea that has been revived more than once.

From the point of view of development the period of Government control was not completely sterile; various committees were set up to examine matters of common interest to the railways. The design of standard locomotives for British railways was one, to which a major contribution was made by R. E. L. Maunsell, Chief Mechanical Engineer of the South Eastern and Chatham Railway who had become CME of the government-sponsored Railway Executive Committee during World War I. Another committee examined the possibility of converting the home railway system to the Continental loading-gauge, to facilitate the circulation of European rolling stock via the cross-Channel train ferries developed during the war. However, when the committee had calculated the enormous cost of converting the SE&CR alone, the idea was promptly dropped! The shortcomings of that company's system, with its load-gauge restrictions and the limited axle-loads which its bridges and track would bear, were to become one of the many problems which confronted the new Southern management.

In 1923, the Southern began the task of combining the three separate organisations of the London & South Western, the London, Brighton & South Coast and the South Eastern & Chatham Railways, plus some minor companies into one body. The task involved the kind of upheaval with which railway staff have more recently become familiar. For the first year there were three General Managers, an arrangement which enabled the three eminent title-holders of the constituent companies jointly to oversee the amalgamation and conveniently allowed two of them to carry on until due for retirement, leaving Mr H. A., later Sir Herbert, Walker of the LSWR to reign supreme from 1924 onwards. Geographically, the Southern divided itself into three sections, Eastern, Central and Western, corresponding approximately to the former company territories, and into five administrative divisions, London (East), London (Central), London (West), Southern (Southampton) and Western (Exeter). As the smallest of the Four Groups, the Southern retained much of the atmosphere of a pre-1923 company. Any part of the system, except west of Exeter, could be visited on business without involving a night away from home, and all the officers could regularly meet one another. Headquarters meetings were held in the committee-rooms in the Charing Cross Hotel, where month by month the General Manager was to hold his Traffic Officers Conference, attended by all divisional (later, district) officers to keep them in the picture.

The Southern was singular in having a one-word title to adorn its locomotives and rolling-stock, and its letter headings!

The selection of a Chief Mechanical Engineer was not difficult to resolve. R. W. Urie of the LSWR was sixty-eight years of age and on the verge of retirement. He had been CME at Eastleigh since Dugald Drummond's death in 1912 and was to leave some excellent locomotives for the Southern including the twenty 4-6-os which were to become the basis of the King Arthur class. He favoured the simple six-coupled locomotive with two large outside cylinders; no fewer than twelve designs of 4-6-0 were prepared in outline, with variations on wheel and cylinder sizes, as well as three possible 2-6-os in appearance like foreshortened H15 4-6-os. A fine 4-8-0 with 5ft 1in coupled wheels and a tractive effort of 30,555 lb had been proposed as far back as 1914 (*see pages 20–21*). L. B. Billinton of the LBSC was 39 years of age; he had served overseas with the rank of Lt-Col during World War I and his absence from the railway scene, and his experience, which was limited to his own company, could not have been to his ultimate advantage. R. E. L. Maunsell, on the other hand, was a mature 54 years of age, having been CME of the SEC since 1913 and, more importantly, of the Railway Executive. With his prominence in the profession and his experience on other railways before going to the SEC, his appointment caused no surprise. L. B. Billinton accepted compensation terms, and a 'handsome piece of presentation plate' from his staff, and retired to live the rest of his life in the country, in Sussex.

Thus, the locomotive engineer who was in due course responsible for the Arthurs, Schools and Nelsons was Richard Edward Lloyd Maunsell, the son of a Dublin lawyer and a graduate of Trinity College, Dublin, two influences which were to make him a first-class administrator. His training as an engineer took place on the Great Southern & Western Railway of Ireland, a company which perforce maintained its locomotive and rolling stock on a limited budget and where Maunsell no doubt learned the importance of careful costing, and of a policy of make-do-and-mend. After a spell of locomotive running experience on the Lancashire & Yorkshire Railway as Shedmaster at Fleetwood, Maunsell followed the custom of many young engineers in those days and took a post on one of the railways in the Commonwealth, in his case on the East Indian Railway. He became the District Locomotive Superintendent at Asansol, the author's grandfather then being the DLS at Allahabad, and in India the difficult conditions under which locomotives operated, climatic and otherwise, imprinted upon his mind the assets of simplicity and utter reliability in design. Rudyard Kipling's story of 'The Bold 'Prentice'* well portrays the Indian railway scene.

Maunsell returned home to be Locomotive, Carriage & Wagon Superintendent of the GS&W, and thence to Ashford as CME of the SEC.

Maunsell was a thoroughly practical locomotive man; humble in his unpretentiousness and ready to delegate to his assistants. With these qualities, and with an Irish twinkle in his eye, he made an excellent leader and the men he picked to work under him stayed loyally with him throughout his time on the Southern.

The burden which fell on his shoulders during the formative years of the Southern Railway was a heavy one because of continual pressure from the General Manager and the Board toward fulfilment of great schemes. The need to produce electric multiple-units in ever-increasing numbers brought unprecedented design and production problems, and some ingenious conversions of steam stock. By 1938 there were over 3,000 coaches of electric stock, a tenfold increase over 1923; during the 1930s much of it was newly-built corridor stock for the main-line extensions to Brighton, Worthing, Eastbourne and Portsmouth. The decisions about stock requirements were not always reached with a generous time allowance for construction before the publicly-announced opening dates; in fact it became a standing joke amongst the workshop staff that almost impossible target dates were set in order to keep everybody's noses to the grindstone. Maunsell made it a point of honour that his rolling stock must be ready in good time to start the new services, and it always was, though there would be a last-minute scramble to find missing bits and pieces. At any rate, when changes in detail design were proposed by other interested departments including the General Manager's, after building had started, Maunsell was a man to put his foot down firmly and say 'no' to such interference.

The steam locomotive stock was in poor shape in 1923. Before he could concentrate on new locomotives of his own design, Maunsell had to draw up a programme for giving all the existing ones a thorough overhaul and to that end to use his available workshop facilities to the best advantage. As events turned out, Maunsell's contribution in new designs was on a small scale compared with the

*Land and Sea Tales, Rudyard Kipling. Macmillan & Co.

opportunities afforded to his colleagues on the other group companies to replace the old with the new. Electrification, and everything to do with it by way of new stations and signalling, received priority in capital expenditure, and the steam locomotive side of the organisation on the Southern soon became the Cinderella, so far as money was concerned. Much ingenuity was expended in modifying and rebuilding older locomotives which, in retrospect, would have been better written off.

The strain upon Maunsell eventually told on his health and after two long illnesses he retired in 1937. When approached on the eve of his retirement, regarding the choice of a parting gift from his staff, he demurred: he wanted no expensive presentation, no silver plate or the traditional mantel clock. It would please him, however, to be given albums of photographs of his assistants, managers and foremen.

In the year of his retirement the direct line to Portsmouth was electrified. For it, he was responsible for the first main-line electric units incorporating the innovation of nose-end gangways. Thirty-four years afterwards the 4-COR units were replaced by more modern stock on the Portsmouth line, but were still running, with the original and wholly satisfactory design of gangway. It would have pleased him, almost as much as the survival of one of his steam locomotives, as an example of value for money, and of faithful service. These were the keynotes of his own personal conduct. When appointing his principal assistants in the early years, he said to one of them, Lionel Lynes, "I expect you will either stay with me for a month, or thirty years!" All his officers stayed with him.

The Southern's Inheritance
of Locomotives

When William Stroudley became the Locomotive Superintendent of the London, Brighton & South Coast Railway in 1870, it possessed 233 locomotives made up of no fewer than seventy-two different types. During his twenty years in office he succeeded in enlarging the total stock but, by a process of standardisation, confined it to a mere seven classes.

In 1923, the Southern Railway inherited from its constituent companies a total of 2,281 locomtives made up of 125 different classes, with an average age of 28 years. A picture of the types of locomotive in service at the amalgamation may be gained by categorising them by wheel-arrangement (omitting a few odd ones) thus:

Tender Locomotives				Tank Locomotives			
4-6-0	73	4-4-0	606	4-8-0T	4	0-6-0T	188
2-6-0	30	0-4-2	116	4-6-4T	7	0-6-4T	5
0-6-0	340	4-2-2-0	6	4-6-2T	7	4-4-2T	120
4-4-2	11			2-6-4T	1	0-4-4T	464
				0-6-2T	134	0-4-2T	112

Maunsell hoped, at one stage, to replace a large proportion of the older locomotives by nine standard types of his own, which between them would employ only five patterns of boiler; these were to be:

Tender Locomotives

Wheel Arrangement	Class	Traffic Type
4-8-0		Mineral*
4-6-0	Lord Nelson	Passenger
4-6-0	King Arthur	Passenger
4-4-0	Schools	Passenger
4-6-0	H15	Mixed
2-6-0	U	Mixed
4-6-0	S15	Goods
2-6-0	N	Goods

*not built.

Tank Locomotive

Wheel Arrangement	Class	Traffic Type
0-8-0T	Z	Shunting

The opportunity to fulfil this plan was denied to Maunsell and when he departed, in 1937, the Southern stock of 1,814 locomotives still included over 70 classes. Although he contributed 340 new locomotives, the average age had risen to 32 years!

Between 1923 and 1938, the average age of the tender locomotives rose from 25 to 28 years, and that of the tank locomotives from 30 to 38½ years.

The main reason for the survival of the veterans has already been mentioned; another reason was the trade slump of the early 1930s which caused proposals for new designs to be held in abeyance. Among the victims was Maunsell's Pacific, an enlarged Lord Nelson later re-drafted as a three-cylinder 2-6-2, and a 4-8-0 freight locomotive. Other victims of the slump were the managerial staff who had to accept a 2½% reduction in their salaries!

Between 1932 and 1937 only 100 new locomotives were built. Twenty Q class 0-6-0 tender locomotives were built in 1938 to Maunsell's design, after his retirement. The medium-sized 0-6-0s, such as the Wainwright C class and the Drummond 700 class, played a useful role on the freight workings and the Qs were intended to cover withdrawals of the older 0-6-0s as they reached a condition otherwise involving expensive repairs. But the threat of war made scrapping inadvisable, and brought a further reprieve for the veterans.

The preponderence of 4-4-0 tender locomotives at the amalgamation reflected the general standard of loads and speeds on the Southern lines and the extent to which passenger trains were made up of timber-built non-corridor bogie coaches and even six-wheelers. It is true that another main-line company, the Midland, had remained a '4-4-0' line but it had an ample number of locomotives with which to double-head the heavier trains. Other companies were well provided with 4-6-0s whereas of the 73 4-6-0s in the new Southern stock, all ex-LSWR, only 20 were suitable for the express work. Twenty-five were Drummond four-cylinder machines built for passenger work but down-graded to freight work because of poor design features.

Eight-coupled freight locomotives, again plentiful elsewhere, did not exist on the Southern. There was indeed no heavy mineral traffic to justify them and the few Robinson ex-ROD 2-8-0s which were on trial on the LSWR in 1920, with a view to purchase of more, were not acquired because of their limited usefulness. Not until 1943, with the arrival of the wartime Austerity 2-8-0s, could Southern enginemen enjoy handling eight-coupleds with excellent adhesion and brake power.

More numerous than the 4-4-0s were the passenger tank engines, indicating the amount of local, and short-distance, passenger services, and branch lines. For that kind of work there was little advantage in fitting them with later developments such as super-heaters and piston valves. Almost without exception they were reliable and easy to maintain, and they continued at work un-molested, long after the Southern Railway era.

In the early years of the LMS and the LNER, the transfer of loco-motive types from one section to another produced some interesting results by way of comparative trials, and incidentally the claim that certain types were best suited to the territory of their origin was exposed as a fallacy. The pooling of resources also enabled the avail-able locomotive stock to be utilised to the best advantage. So far as the Southern was concerned there were many difficulties in the way of so doing. The loading gauge on the Eastern section was less generous than on the Central and the Western sections. More serious still, in constructing the South Eastern and the London, Chatham & Dover Railways the depth allowed between the track and the formation level, for ballasting, was in time to prove entirely inade-quate for the increasing train speeds and weights of locomotives. The shortcomings of the permanent way in Kent were destined to be demonstrated dramatically by a number of derailments of the River class 2-6-4 tanks, culminating in 1927 with the disaster at Riverhead, near Sevenoaks, and considerable expenditure on the track, and on the underbridges, had to be incurred on the three main routes to Dover, via Chatham, via Maidstone and via Tonbridge.

The composite loading gauge, to which nearly all new Southern locomotives and rolling stock were built, was dictated by that of the Eastern section. Ex-LBSC and ex-LSWR locomotives required for use on that section which did not conform to the composite gauge had first to have their cab-roofs and footsteps cut back, denoted by a yellow triangle on the buffer beam. Even tighter restrictions applied to, and still remain on, the Tonbridge–Hastings line.

Companies like the LBSC which used the Westinghouse air brake were in the minority, and the vacuum brake became the standard throughout the country, although the LSWR and LBSC electric stock fitted with the air brake retained it. Fifty years later, the air brake was to be used on all Southern Region stock. The ex-LBSC air-braked locomotives represented a considerable proportion of the locomotive stock and it was essential that most of them, at any rate, should be able to work vacuum-braked trains. It was not possible simply to strip them of the air brake and replace it by vacuum, as all the brake rigging was designed for operation by air cylinders, which occupied less space than vacuum cylinders anyway. The solution, which of course took time, lay in the fitting of ex-LBSC locomotives with vacuum ejectors and with dual brake controls. The locomotive brakes remained air-operated, and by means of a proportional valve the activation of the driver's air brake control also applied to the same degree the vacuum brakes on the train. The necessary proportional valve was devised and patented by a Brighton Works foreman, E. M. Jackson.

Other differences were not always welcomed when engines were transferred to other areas. A left-hand driving position was standardised on the LSW and LBSC, but the SEC locomotives were right-hand drive. In keeping with the locomotive controls, the signals of each company had been sited in positions where they would be best seen from the driver's side. Drivers eventually got used to the existence of both lh and rh drive types, which persisted to the end of steam, although the opposites were occasionally the cause of minor collisions when two locomotives moving in the same direction in a marshalling or locomotive yard met at points, neither driver having seen the other! The arrangement was much more disliked by the firemen, not all of whom could readily become ambidextrous in wielding a shovel accurately. When, for instance, ex-LSWR 4-4-0s of classes T9, L11 and L12 were drafted on to the Eastern section to ease a shortage of power, fireman and driver would be found occupying the same side of the footplate, with obvious friction.

Differences in the direction of rotation, clockwise or anti-clockwise, of control handles proved to be something of a menace. Regulators, hand-brake wheels and blower-valves could be hurriedly, and so incorrectly, operated, hence the kind of incident which occurred at Nine Elms when an ex-Brighton tank went through the boundary wall into 'The Brooklands Arms'. When the 0-8-0 tank engine *Hecate* was acquired from the Kent and East Sussex Railway, it had a reversing lever which one pulled back for forward travel and vice versa: immediate modifications were made before any walls were demolished. Blower valves had to be standardised to open

Proposed Urie 4-8-0 freight locomotive

clockwise, and the handles clearly marked, since any mistake in the use of the blower could result in a 'blow-back' with possibly fatal burns.

The Brighton tank engines of the E classes were popular shunting engines because of the air brakes, hence their longevity and their eventual appearance on all divisions. By contrast, some of the LSW G6 shunting engines relied upon the hand brake alone until the Southern got around to providing them all with vacuum brakes. Just as primitive were the Brighton A1 and D1 tanks, C3 0-6-0 goods engines, and others, which possessed only crosshead-driven feed pumps, and not until 1930–32 were they all equipped with injectors: meantime only ex-Brighton enginemen could manage them and they were definitely not types to be sent elsewhere than to Central section depots! Even though most engines were straightfoward enough to drive, there were niceties of handling, and of all the types those which took longest to become accustomed to were Drummond's engines. The Drummond steam reverser was of somewhat small dimensions so that it could be fitted neatly out of sight between the frames and close to the reversing shaft and valve gear. In contrast, the Ashford engines used the massive Stirling steam reverser,

WATER 5200 GALLONS

3'7"DIA

9' 4½" — 6' 6" — 6' 0" — 6' 6" — 4' 7⅝"

19' 0"

57' 1½" TOTAL WHEELBASE

OVERALL

28T. 16C   28T. 14C

NE & TENDER. 140T. 0C IN WORKING ORDER   57T. 10C

mounted outside, as large as, and often mistaken for, a Westinghouse air pump. It was a most dependable device, whereas Drummond's was finicky and temperamental and if its various cocks, glands and leather washers were not serviced by skilled fitters, it would alter the cut-off or change from foregear to backgear on its own.

Incidentally the standard of workmanship of running shed fitters, and the educational standard required to pass as a driver, were highest on the LSWR, largely the legacy of Drummond's interest in the Mutual Improvement Classes by which the staff gained their technical knowledge—in their off-duty hours, moreover.

The injector controls on Drummond's T9 and other classes of 4-4-0 were, unusually, on the floor of the cab, where they could be set by a tap of the heel. The fireman could simultaneously adjust the injector steam supply and have a hand free to steady himself. It worked well, and enabled the fireman to set an injector working without excessive back-rushes of steam and water from the injector overflow. But the heel-tapping required practice. Drummond himself could not have ridden on his own locomotives or he would surely have improved the weather protection of his cabs. As it was, the T9 cab roof only partially covered the space between engine and tender, and the cab-side cutaways were unnecessarily large. There were no doors: only a chain between engine and tender to prevent the crew from falling overboard. When the Stewarts Lane (Eastern section) men saw their first King Arthurs, they promptly dubbed the T9s the 'Queen Annes'.

Another difference between the pre-Southern companies, which affected locomotive design and handling techniques, lay in the varying types and sources of coal. In order to minimise the cost of coal insofar as haulage charges were involved, the choice of certain collieries as sources of supply was affected by geography. The LSWR used mainly Welsh coal, which was distributed over its system via the Severn Tunnel and Salisbury, whereas for the LBSC and SEC coal from the Midlands and Yorkshire would travel via the West London or Widened lines. Regular travellers used to claim that they could tell which railway they were riding on, simply by the smell of the coal! The Midlands and Yorkshire coals tended to be gassy, quick-burning coals, with a high residue of ash. This type of fuel required a grate with ample spacing between the firebars to allow the ash to fall into an ash-pan of ample proportions. Conversely, Welsh coal made very little ash, and LSWR fireboxes were shallow and the firebars closely spaced to minimise loss of unburnt fuel into the ashpan. Here again were differences in design which brought complications, not only in fuel supplies to locomotive depots but also in the quantity of ashpan and smokebox refuse which could limit the time a locomotive could spend in traffic between visits to the ashpits.

After amalgamation, the Southern continued to use the same sources of coal supplies, except that the Kent coalfields were by then producing good quality coal from Chislet and Snowdown, which was sent to Eastern section depots, for main-line work. Betteshanger, a cheap, low-grade Kent coal, was sent all over the system for the exclusive use by shunting locomotives. The tall, hopper-type coaling plants installed at Stewarts Lane, Feltham and Nine Elms were for preference supplied with hard Yorkshire coal as it did not readily pulverise when tipped into a 400-ton capacity hopper.

The price paid per ton of locomotive coal was higher in the South than elsewhere. Figures for 1908 published by the railway companies show that the LSWR was paying 17s 9d, the LBSC 17s 11d and the SEC 15s 9d per ton, whereas the other companies were paying an average of 10s to 12s per ton. The price paid by the Southern companies was partly due to the longer haulage from the collieries* and partly because passenger train working required better grades of

*The Kent coalfield was a later development.

coal than freight train working. In the South the proportion of passenger train miles to freight train miles was of the order of 75% to 25%, whereas in the Midlands and the North the proportion was the other way round.

The cost of fuel was the largest item in the annual expense account of a locomotive department, a matter which the management endeavoured by various means to keep in the minds of enginemen. Prior to 1914 many companies operated a system whereby the drivers received a bonus when the locomotive allocated to them achieved a better-than-average coal consumption. The system encouraged a certain amount of fiddling, whereby the men who loaded the coal on the engines would be bribed to falsify their bookings, or coal would be taken off another engine or from the stacks which were held in reserve at the locomotive depots. Attempts were made to discourage malpractices; for example by whitewashing coal on tenders and in stack so that any interference could be noticed, and in the end the bonus system fell into such disrepute that it was dropped; moreover, it became inoperable with the growing practice of common-user locomotives. On the Southern, there continued to be published at the locomotive depots, until 1939, a monthly statement of the coal consumption the individual locomotives used on main-line passenger work, but the figures as between one locomotive and another could vary for so many reasons outside the enginemen's control that their publication was merely a general reminder for economy.

With the train loads and speeds which prevailed at about the time of the amalgamation, a figure of 30–35lb per mile could be expected from locomotives working passenger trains; on freight trains the consumption would range from 60–90lb per mile, according to conditions. The lowest averages prevailed in the South, with little heavy freight traffic.

On the SEC and the LBSC, few locomotives had boilers with a grate area of 20sq ft and over. An increase on this figure had been a feature of post-1918 rebuilds such as the Ashford D1s and E1s and the Brighton B4X. Notable exceptions were the LBSC Atlantics with 31sq ft and the I3 with 23¾sq ft, both very successful. Coal economy was not improved by the need to thrash smaller locomotives: Holcroft recalls that the spark-throwing by Stirling B1s and F1s rivalled that associated with Crewe locomotives!

On the LSWR, Drummond had, as early as 1899, provided his passenger 4-4-0s of classes T9, S11 and L12, with 24sq ft of grate, increased to 27sq ft on the D15s and 31sq ft on his 4-6-0s. The LBSC Remembrance class Baltics were limited by other design considerations to 26.7sq ft, so that when rebuilt as tender engines in 1934 for use on the Western Section, they did not rank much above the Drummond T14s in performance.

Along with generous grate areas Drummond, with an eye to economy, like the true Scot he was, equipped his locomotives with various coal-saving devices; steam driers in the smokebox; cross water-tubes in the firebox; and water-heaters in the tender. He also enforced a rigid surveillance over the enginemen to make sure they handled the controls in the most economical way, with wide-open regulators and short cut-offs for maximum expansion; hence it is not surprising that the overall coal consumption per train mile was lowest on the LSW, as the following figures, again for the year 1908, show:

LSW   46.9lb per mile
LBSC   51.4 lb per mile
SEC   59.9lb per mile.

On the other hand, Drummond's devices were expensive to fit and maintain, so what was gained on the swings was lost on the round-abouts. The same conclusion was ultimately reached, in the closing years of steam in Britain, that complicated equipment, which theoretically saved money by lower fuel consumption, cost in one way or another more than it saved.

A Crisis: Locomotives in Travail

A young engine cleaner had often to undergo some form of initiation ceremony, such as being daubed with soot, after which he would be held under the outlet of a water-column while somebody turned the valve. The young Southern Railway was likewise destined to suffer a cold douche, in the form of criticism and ridicule by the popular press.

During its first year, all seemed set for a prosperous future. Passenger traffic was buoyant, with 59 million passenger journeys in 1923, representing a 26 per cent increase over the total for the constituent companies in 1913. Competition from private cars and from air transport to the Continent was negligible. Although few people enjoyed holidays with pay, the South Coast was a popular venue for day trips and good business was done with excursion trains. The staff of the three companies carried on much as before with their own methods of working whilst the new management, seemingly in no great haste, reshaped its organisation and centralised its headquarters at Waterloo Station. But the post-war public was not inclined to be as tolerant as it had been of delays and discomforts.

Post-war reductions in the length of the working day in offices and workshops had the effect of concentrating commuter traffic in the morning and evening and over-taxing the steam-hauled suburban services.

On the Eastern (SECR) section, as yet untouched by electrification, the suburban train consisted of six-wheelers drawn by an 0-4-4T. On the main line there was no corridor stock apart from a few boat-train sets built at Ashford in 1922, and some LSWR stock had to be hastily transferred, to form trains with the odd Pullman car in the rake. Some Drummond engines were also sent on loan. South-Western officials, already put out by the appointment of ex-SECR men to top jobs, including the Chief Mechanical and Chief Civil Engineers, regarded such loans as the penalty of an enforced marriage with an inferior Kentish railway system. On the busiest day of the Easter rush in 1924, of the 36 down boat trains from Charing Cross and Cannon Street, the majority were formed of non-corridor, non-lavatory coaches, some with nothing better to haul them than elderly M3 4-4-0s or Stirling O class goods engines with 5ft 2in driving wheels and 140lb pressure. The annual exodus of South Londoners to the hop-fields of Kent drew forth the roughest specimens of South Eastern stock; the customers did not complain, since there was ample room under the hard seats for the concealment of ticketless families. Regular passengers were convinced that hop-pickers' trains could be found in general circulation!

Conditions were less Dickensian on the Brighton line, although at holiday times a trip to the seaside was likely to be made in suburban stock behind a Billinton E4 0-6-2 tank with stops for the loco to take water and for the passengers to relieve themselves. The LBSCR had only eleven Atlantics, seven Baltics and the two 4-6-2 tanks *Abergavenny* and *Bessborough* in their front rank: Newhaven boat trains and the 'Sunny South Express' to and from the North via Willesden might have nothing better than a Gladstone B1 class 0-4-2. At any rate the Brighton management had ambitious plans for further electrification on the 11,000v overhead system. When the Southern decided to standardise 600v third-rail traction, these plans were, naturally, held up. But such was the urgency to cope with commuter traffic that extensions of the overhead wire were made to outer suburbia and it was not until 1929 that conversion to third-rail had been completed on the Central (Brighton) section.

On the Western section the LSWR at the time of the grouping had, to quote M. P. White, 'firmly laid the foundations of a service which was frequent, regular and punctual. Everywhere the average was excellent, and there was nothing spectacular either in speed or waywardness. These were the foundations upon which the Southern built up its own distinctive tradition.' Before the Kaiser war ended, the LSWR started to rehabilitate itself with new locomotives and rolling stock. By 1923 there was the latest thing in hump marshalling yards at Feltham, and in the reconstructed Waterloo Station the LSWR had the largest station in Britain, handling the largest number of trains, 1,034 daily. South-Western men would have much preferred to join forces with the Great Western. East of Waterloo there was that 'Hornby' railway—the name under which the Meccano firm had just put its new 'O gauge' train sets on the market. "How far is it to Brighton?" asked an LSWR man of an LBSCR man who boasted of Baltics and Pullmans, "only 51 miles! Why, we fly-shunt further than that!"

At Victoria, a dividing wall separating the SEC and the LBSC portions of the station, demolished during 1924, was somehow symbolic of the many obstacles to be overcome before the Southern could operate as one railway, and one team. The staff continued to wear the uniforms and badges of the old companies. Many of them had not long been demobilised from the Forces. Others were recent recruits in place of the railwaymen who had lost their lives. Following the war, the railway companies and the railway unions had come together and drawn up conditions of service and 'who-does-what' agreements which were to apply nationally; they also produced an admirable and workable constitution for negotiations between management and staff at local and regional levels. Nevertheless, unification of the conditions could not be achieved overnight. The introduction of an eight-hour, instead of a ten-hour, day for railwaymen also involved additional recruits.

The constituent companies had competing services to towns served by more than one of them, and to eliminate the duplication of the longer and slower routes the Southern re-cast its timetable.

There is, time has proved, no quicker way to upset the travelling public than by altering the pattern of train service to which they have become accustomed, however good a case may be made for changes. In 1924, such changes were construed as lack of consideration for the public by a new railway monopoly. The railway companies were largely to blame for their traditional aloofness toward public criticism; they made little attempt to foster relations with press and public. It was, anyway, impossible to please everybody all the time.

The Southern soon came to realise the value of public goodwill, and to create a new department to take care of 'Advertising and Publicity'. Its first task was to combat the press attacks which increased in volume and virulence towards the end of 1924, seizing upon every minor delay or incident out of which to make headlines. The Southern was an easy target; it had been a bad summer: trains crawling behind time or standing motionless in mid-section, trains ending up at the wrong station or not starting through lack of engines. A shortage of seating had not been helped by the withdrawal of coaching stock for conversion into electric trains. Above all, it was trouble with the locomotives that really upset the apple-cart. Taking each locomotive failure as the loss of more than five minutes on a passenger train or replacement of the locomotive before completing the journey, there were 267 failures in the month of August 1924; moreover one may guess that, things being what they were, not every case was reported. Eight locomotive failures a day were bound to play havoc with the timetable, and the figures did not include 'non-mechanical casualties' attributed to mismanagement by enginemen, shortage of water in boiler or tender, shortage of coal, boiler priming (overdue for washout, perhaps), slipping and over-loading. There were late starts due to 'Awaiting locomotive' or 'Late arrival off previous service', which might be the reaction from a failure, or was, quite likely, the impounding of locomotives by traffic disruption at terminal stations, thus delaying coaling and watering for the next trip. No wonder the Southern operators welcomed the electric multiple-unit! The worst culprits amongst a host of causes of mechanical failure were the overheated big-ends, slidebars and eccentrics. The use of white-metal of inferior quality, a legacy of war-time, had something to do with bearing troubles but even at that comparatively late stage in the art of design the reliability of big-ends was far from perfect. Drummond's inside big-ends were notorious and only by fitting additional felt oiling pads into recesses in the bearing surface could a reasonable mileage be obtained without overheating. Next on the list were leaking or broken boiler tubes: again, many boilers were overdue for complete re-tubing. In the six years between the armistice and 1924 it had not been possible to give every locomotive a general overhaul in works. Other causes high on the list were overheated axleboxes, injector and feed pump defects, leaking pipes and joints, followed closely by failures due to loose fittings. The steel wheel pounding on the steel rail produces vibrations guaranteed to shake loose nuts and bolts not firmly secured by locking washers and split pins. A fresh hazard had appeared, in that bits that fell off were liable to cause fireworks in contact with the conductor rail. A vigorous campaign against preventable failures and the introduction of new locomotives gradually brought about an improvement. In August 1927 the total failures for the busiest month of the year had fallen to 93 compared with the 267 cases in 1924. Whatever action could be taken to improve the condition of existing locomotives for 1925 it was obvious that new express passenger locomotives must be procured at once, hence the directors urged Maunsell to finalise a design which could be produced quickly in some numbers, and to find a locomotive building firm which could execute a contract at short notice. The locomotive drawing offices were at once put on overtime to prepare specifications for tendering by outside industry. The King Arthurs were on the way.

A promise of better things to come was made by Sir Herbert Walker at a meeting at the Savoy Hotel in January 1925, to which representatives of local authorities on the Southern system had been invited. Sir Herbert admitted, with some candour, that there had been serious shortcomings, and his announcement that £10 million

Top: 'David and Goliath'—a favourite theme of pre-group railway publicity photographs—L. Billinton's Baltic and Stroudley's Terrier in 1914.

Above: Drummond's first four-cylinder 4-6-0, No 330, at Waterloo, 1905. Note 'upside down' Walschaerts gear to outside cylinders.

Top: A fine view of No 720, Drummond's four-cylinder double-single on test in 1905, with contemporary LSWR main-line stock.

Above: Close-up of No 720 at Nine Elms fitted with indicating gear, and as fitted with 1905 large boiler

Top: Maunsell's River class No A791 *River Adur*. It was built in 1925 and converted to U class 2-6-0 in 1928. Tanks and bunkers were later used for Z class 0-8-OTs.

Above: Urie's N15 4-6-0 No 749 as built, September 1922./*BR*

Top: Drummond's G14 4-6-0 No 453, built 1908, rebuilt 1925.

Above: Maunsell's rebuild of Drummond 4-6-0 No 448, 1925.

One of Drummond's last 'Paddleboats', No 461 showing deep splashers and port-hole access to expansion link.

'Paddleboat' No 460 as running in SR days, with improved access to motion./*Author*

Top: No 451 with indicator shelters for 1925 tests./Locomotive Publishing Co

Above: NB Loco Co Arthur No 767 *Sir Valence* as built, 1925.

NB Loco Co Arthur No 772 *Sir Percivale* with German pattern of smoke deflector plates.

No 767 working a down boat train in 1929 at Petts Wood. The train is made up of SECR 1922 stock with six-wheeled brake and luggage van, 'birdcage' lookout./*H. C. Casserley*

Top: No. 795 *Sir Dinadin* with six-wheel tender as built in 1926./*BR*

Above: No 797 *Sir Blamor de Ganis,* new at Brighton in 1926, with I3 class behind and Terrier in front./*H. Gordon Tidey*

Below: Smoke deflector experiments, 1927. No 450 *Sir Kay*/*LPC*

was to be spent on modernisation was sufficient to silence the opposition.

On the operating methods of the railway Sir Herbert Walker was to impose strict disciplines. All trains, loaded or empty, and all regular light engine movements had to be worked to timings as published to the staff in the Working Time-Tables. No recovery allowances were incorporated in train schedules, as they were regarded as conducive to an easy-going attitude on the part of drivers; to minimise interference from permanent-way works the Civil Engineer had first to seek approval for any temporary speed restrictions and their number was limited on any given route. All additional trains, whether revenue-earning or for some railway purpose, such as ballast-carrying or coaches going to a works for repairs, had to be shewn either in a weekly printed notice or else on a stencilled notice to be circulated 24 hours beforehand. The notices were delivered to all stations, signalboxes, loco depots and to anyone else likely to be concerned, eg inspectors of every rank and interest.

The running of an extra train at a few hours' notice, by telephonic arrangement, was countenanced only in certain circumstances. Sir Herbert's dictum was 'Plan Your Traffic'; a shaft which was aimed particularly at those station and yard masters who would, by lack of foresight, want to have their own yards cleared of surplus stock immediately by an extra train which might merely move the congestion from A to B and interfere with passenger traffic in doing so. Any extra trains likely to be required on odd days—for example, Ocean Liner trains—were allotted Q or ghost pathways in the WTT which kept clear of any other trains.

Sir Herbert did not hold with the use of Traffic Control Offices, believing that thereby initiative was taken away from outdoor staff in immediate contact with the running of trains and transferred to clerks in offices. When war came in 1939, it became essential to have some form of control in order to arrange trains at a moment's notice, though out of respect for Sir Herbert, they were not termed Controls but Train Supervision Offices.

This apparent prejudice against the telephone, as an adjunct to laziness, or as a potential cause of misunderstandings, certainly resulted in the survival of an antiquated telephone system. A limited number of direct telephone lines radiated from Waterloo to manual exchanges at some of the principal stations, but otherwise there existed a network of omnibus circuits, notorious for the number of inquisitive ears likely to overhear conversations, and for the poor quality of audibility. By official circulars staff were from time to time urged never to use the telephone as a substitute, time permitting, for written communications!

In one respect the omnibus telephone system was unrivalled, before the era of the transistor radio, and that was in the transmission of news; the winner of the Derby was circulated within minutes of the race! It was also used to warn of the presence of officialdom in the area. The late A. Earle Edwards used to recount how, as an assistant district officer, he had reproved a signalman for being on duty in an unshaven condition, thereby incurring himself a nickname derived from a much-advertised brand of shaving cream, as he was soon to discover. He arrived at a country signalbox by car and, the signalman being engaged, he answered a call on the telephone circuit to hear a voice say "Look out, Jack, old 'Shavex' is around!"

West of Salisbury there was, until 1939, no trunk telephone line. Business was still transacted by the single-needle telegraph, using the Railway Clearing House Code. Coded telegrams were the principal means of communicating with the other railway companies. The code-word BOYNE was known to locomotive men, as a warning that no water was available at a particular station—eg 'Boyne Basingstoke'. 'Clyde Basingstoke' meant that water had been restored. On the occasion of an annual office outing, it was customary to send a 'Boyne' telegram to the place at which the party was due to take lunch-time refreshment! Other locomotive code words included CHENG for changing engines, NORUN for a failure and, with less obvious derivation, COLORADO to order a pilot engine and HEBREW for a train with an assisting engine.

To keep station, signalbox and office clocks correct, before the days of the BBC, a time-signal used to be transmitted over the telephone and telegraph system from headquarters at 10am each morning: the further the station from London, the less accurately the clocks were liable to read. Some drivers used to try and time their trains by reading station clocks en route, for not every driver possessed a watch. By a curious anomaly, guards were supplied with watches to enable them to compile their train journals, but drivers were not, and the custom remains the same on BR today. The majority of drivers, anyway, preferred to have their own watches, and at every locomotive depot there was always somebody who made a lucrative hobby out of watch and clock repairing. The Southern gingered up its timekeeping by Lost Time Tickets requiring drivers to answer for as little as one minute lost. A driver would do almost anything rather than put pen to paper.

New Designs

In attempting to discern the pedigree of the Arthurs, Schools and Nelsons, we find ourselves tracing through the threads of a tangled web. These threads lead us back to earlier engines from which experience had been gained and to designers whose ideas had influenced the parent CME. Interwoven with these threads are others which represent the economic circumstances ruling at the time, the developments of the traffic, the strength of the civil engineering works, and the mechanical equipment possessed by the railway concerned.

In the prosperous days of railways and steam locomotives, engineering journals were able to publish details of a new locomotive in almost every issue. There would be a photograph with the impressive caption 'Designed by Mr C. Y. Lindercock, Locomotive Superintendent, Great Smashem & Cheatham Rly.' In the following month would appear an article on the 'fine 4-4-0 express locomotive designed by Mr C. O. Upling of the Long, Slow and Winding Rly.' Careful comparison of their principal dimensions might reveal that there were only slight differences in the sizes of the working parts, albeit each locomotive conformed outwardly to the parent designer's, or company's, distinctive styling which prevented anyone from thinking that one was a copy of the other. Both were almost certainly a modified or slightly enlarged version of an earlier design. There was nothing wrong in that. The steam locomotive grew up by a gradual process and few designers could afford to risk any dramatic experiments. But there was a curious isolationism about the railway design offices. They could have learned so many useful lessons from one another. Books of locomotive diagrams supplied to senior officers would carry stern warnings, such as the one in our Eastleigh diagram book: 'This book is issued to Mr ...... on the understanding that it is for his personal use only and must not be lent to anyone else on any pretext whatever. The information it contains is confidential and must not be passed on.'

Swindon had the reputation of being the most secretive place. Yet there was little that could not be discovered about GWR locomotives by some mild espionage, and one hardly need go so far as that when GWR locomotives could be observed in action in half the counties of England. A knowledgable observer could spot the long travel of the valve spindle as one of Churchward's engines moved off, and hear the sharpness of the exhaust. Passing at speed, the barely-audible beats and the wide sweep of the connecting rods gave clear indication of the high expansion ratio. The higher than average boiler pressure of 225lb was a published figure. On each side of the smokebox, large steam pipes took a direct route to the outside steam chests. No patents covered these features. Swindon locomotives passed daily beneath the windows of Eastleigh drawing office where new locomotives, such as the H15 and N15 4-6-0s, were being designed with short-travel valves, 180lb boiler pressure and indirect steam pipes. The drawing-office staff were ruled in schoolmasterly fashion by a chief draughtsman, who did not expect his staff to venture as far as riding on footplates and was never known to do so himself. Any suggestions from the shop floor or from the running department for alterations to drawings, by improvements, were strongly resented. If the case was a good one, the design would be changed but not in the form originally suggested!

Before the amalgamation five companies possessed dynamometer cars for locomotive road-testing. These were not in everyday use and it is difficult to believe that, had they wanted to do so, other CMEs could not have come to some arrangement to hire one.

The advances in design achieved at Swindon stemmed from Churchward's interest in what other locomotive engineers were doing: the use of higher boiler pressures and long piston strokes in the United States, and in France the fine workmanship put into locomotives working on the compound principle. A generation later, Gresley's 4-6-2s for the Great Northern main-line were inspired by the success of a prototype Pacific built by an American locomotive manufacturer which had distinguished itself on the Pennsylvania Railroad and on the stationary testing plant at Altoona.

Maunsell, too, believed, in his own words, in 'looking around for the best practice'. He mixed as often as possible with fellow engineers, at international railway conferences and at meetings in London of the Civil, Mechanical and Locomotive Engineers Institutions. In his first design, for the SEC, the N class 2-6-0, he acknowledged that the cylinders and long valve-travel had followed the practice of Swindon, on which he went one better by adding a Horwich development, higher superheat temperatures. The new coaches built at Ashford for the Continental boat trains, in 1922, must, he told Lionel Lynes, his carriage and wagon officer, 'ride as well as the London & North Western coaches'—a tall order when the latter were running on the 'finest permanent way in the world', as the LNWR claimed, and the SECR probably had the worst!

Impetus toward collaboration between the railway CMEs had been given when, while the railways were still under government control after World War I, a committee, which included such eminent men as Gresley (GN), Churchward (GW), Fowler (MR) and Hughes (L&Y), was charged with the task of drawing up specifications for standard locomotives. The committee was dissolved after amalgamation, ultimately to come to life again under nationalisation in the form of a design team drawn from all the regions of British Railways. With a few arguable exceptions, the BR standard locomotives incorporated the best features of the locomotives designed during the previous twenty-five years. The leader of the BR design team, E. S. Cox, later wrote* '. . . there finally emerged an end product which exploited nearly all the practical, as distinct from the theoretical, possibilities of steam traction. To such men as Gresley, Maunsell, Stanier, George Ivatt and Riddles the historian must rightly accord the credit for original thought and application which assured its success.'

Before his inception as Southern CME, Maunsell had cast a critical eye over the products of Brighton and Eastleigh. The Brighton school of design was evidently out of touch with the best developments elsewhere; the latest design, the Baltic *Remembrance* class (Plate 1.1.), was a handsome heavyweight. As a tank locomotive it was pointless because it was never used to work fast trains with bunker leading, it was always turned. The Brighton K class 2-6-0 did good work but the Ashford N 2-6-0 did better. Maunsell saw in the Eastleigh N15 4-6-0s many of the good points which long experience had taught him to adopt in his own design policy. Here were some locomotives built for strength and durability, everything about them was accessible and a pit was only needed for ashpan emptying. Both smokeboxes and ashpans were of such a size so that neither needed to be emptied too often of ash and char. There were no gadgets or fancy fittings. The bearings throughout were of generous dimensions. Lubrication of cylinders, valves and axleboxes was provided from the footplate, where the enginemen could control it. Many of the components were standard with other Urie types.

The LSWR had steadily invested in new locomotives throughout most of its history. Between 1918 and 1923, in spite of post-war difficulties, 49 new locomotives had been built, which was more than

*Locomotive Panorama Vol. 2, E. S. Cox, Ian Allan (1966).

the combined output of Ashford and Brighton. Eastleigh Works was the most modern in the country. Its running sheds were generally the best laid out and the best equipped on the Southern. In many ways, the LSWR had more in common with the larger companies north of the Thames; it was financially sound, the civil engineering works had from the beginning been constructed soundly with sufficient capital, and the traffic had shown a steady growth. The originating freight traffic exceeded that of both the LBSCR and SECR put together. It had substantial investments in property and in docks. It was the only Southern company on which through loco-motive workings were long enough to involve the provision of dormitories and lodgings for enginemen, and the only company with a four-track main-line for fifty miles out of London. These were some of the threads mentioned at the beginning of this chapter which had influenced locomotive development.

The first 4-6-0s on the LSWR had been built by Drummond in 1905, the F13 class, with four cylinders. Two inside cylinders beneath the smokebox drove the leading pair of driving wheels, and two outside cylinders were positioned adjacent to the leading coupled wheels to drive the middle pair. The divided-drive arrangement of a four-cylinder engine followed that adapted with the 4-2-2-0 type No 720 produced in 1897. That locomotive had in turn been based, it is held on good authority, upon Webb's LNWR 2-2-2-0 type divided-drive locomotives which had evidently taken Drummond's fancy, not on account of the compound expansion so much as of the free running of uncoupled pairs of driving wheels. Engine No 720 performed less well than the ordinary two-cylinder 4-4-0s but, nothing daunted, Drummond built five more 4-2-2-0s in 1901 with larger boilers. In all his 4-2-2-0s, as with Webb's, the inside and outside cylinders were separated by a length of frame. The stresses set up by the thrusts of separate cylinders caused fatigue cracks in a portion of the frame which could not be made deeper without fouling the bogie wheels. In action, they were temperamental machines. The inside and outside sets of cylinders would operate alternately in and out of phase with one another, which upset the balancing and the even draught on the fire. The engines, Nos 720 and 369–373, became known to the staff as 'Butterflies' because they appeared at work on fine days at the peak of summer traffic, but seldom at other times. Drummond would have been sensible to have rebuilt them as straight two-cylinder 4-4-0s, and one suspects that it was the loss of face which prevented him. George Whale was at the time reverting to two-cylinder 4-4-0s after he succeeded Webb as CME at Crewe.

Drummond was an obstinate Scot and in due time his obstinacy cost the company more money because the five F13 4-6-os cracked their frames in just the same places. Transmitting the drive in that way certainly avoided the concentration of weight and stress on one driving axle and the principle was employed by other engineers. It was the location of the cylinders which caused trouble. A better arrangement was to have the cylinder blocks in line and to divide the drive by differences in the length either of the piston rods or the connecting rods, or both.

Picking holes in the work of past designers, of course, can sound supercilious, so let us hasten to imagine the difficulties that they had to contend with, on the LSWR in particular. The only instrumentation that was available for test purposes was the steam-engine indicator which drew a diagram of the compression and expansion within the cylinder. Alloy steels, case-hardening processes, crack detectors, strain gauges, and so on, were non-existent, or in their infancy. Ultrasonic testing and industrial X-ray photography lay in the future. When parts of a locomotive broke or developed cracks the cause was often a matter of guess-work, the cure to increase the thickness of metal. Engines were allowed to run with cracked spokes, frames, hornblocks and cylinder castings provided that the cracks were marked and regularly inspected by running-shed fitters for any sign of worsening.

Drummond's attempts to produce a successful four-cylinder 4-6-o were examples of trial and error. In chronological order they were:

Nos	Date	Cylinders	Boiler tubes	Firebox Water Tubes	Scrapped or Rebuilt
330–334	1906	16in × 24in	340 × 1$\frac{3}{4}$in	112 × 2$\frac{3}{4}$in	1924–5
335	1907	16$\frac{1}{2}$in × 26in	340 × 1$\frac{3}{4}$in	112 × 2$\frac{3}{4}$in	1914
453–457	1908	15in × 26in	247 × 1$\frac{3}{4}$in	84 × 2$\frac{3}{4}$in	1925
448–452	1910	15in × 26in	247 × 1$\frac{3}{4}$in	84 × 2$\frac{3}{4}$in	1925–7
443–447 458–462	1911–12	15in × 26in	247 × 1$\frac{3}{4}$in	84 × 2$\frac{3}{4}$in	1915–18 (Mods)

Full details are available in reference books. The above changes show that the cylinder sizes were reduced, an indication that the cylinders were at first too large for the boiler's steaming capacity. Although the boilers were reduced in size and in the number of tubes when the cylinders were bored at 15in, the gas flow and the steaming could well have been better in spite of the reduction in heating surfaces.

Original Urie design for a King Arthur as built in 1917. Coupled axle weights were later corrected to 58T 7C.

A NB Loco Co-built type as new.

COAL 5 TONS

WATER 5000 GALL.S

3′ 7″ DIA.

 II′ 6″ 6′ 6″ 6′ 0″ 6′ 6″ 4′ 7⅝″

19′ 0″

6′ 5¼″ OVERALL

TENDER 57T. IC

NDER IN WKG. ORDER 134T. I8C

COAL 5 TONS

WATER 5000 GALL.S

3′ 5½″

3′ 7″ DIA.

II′ 6″ 6′ 6″ 6′ 0″ 6′ 6″ 4′ 7⅝″

19′ 0″

58′ 0″

66′ 5¼″

29T 9C 28T 2C

ENDER IN WKG ORDER I38T. IO C. 57T. IIC

A grate area of 31·5sq ft—larger than on the King Arthur class—was provided on all the engines, and 6ft 0in diam coupled wheels, and 175lb boiler pressure, until the final batch, 443–7 and 458–62, which had 6ft 7in wheels and 200lb pressure. The latter engines had two outside sets of valve gear to operate the four valves, with rocking shafts to the inside valves, and Eastleigh never found a way of setting the valve gear which would give equal port openings on all four valves. By their appearance they looked capable of timing the 'Atlantic Coast Express'; instead they were more suitable to work stopping trains to Basingstoke.

No-one from amongst the ex-LSWR technical staff who was around in Southern days could quite explain the logic behind Drummond's experiments with his 4-6-0s. All agreed, anyway, that the first sixteen belonged to the 'Couldn't-pull-pussy' class. In the last year of his life, in 1912, Drummond reverted to a 4-4-0 type with the excellent D15 class which became for a time the mainstay of the Bournemouth express services. On this same route in 1937 another 4-4-0, the Schools class, was destined to rival the performance of the 4-6-0s.

The Development of the Arthurs

Nobody dared criticise Drummond's engines while he was alive—at least not openly. He held that there were no bad engines of his, only bad enginemen. It did not reach his ears that the initials LSWR on the water-cart tenders of his four-cylinder locomotives stood for 'Lazy Swines Won't Run'. After his death, R. W. Urie rebuilt No 335 to his own H15 design, and was dealing similarly with Nos 330–334 at the time of his retirement. He had financial authority to rebuild Nos 448–457 but had not made up his mind about the details of the conversion. The last ten 'Paddleboats' were destined to survive, with Maunsell modifications, until after World War II except for No 458 blitzed in 1940.

Urie's N15 class 4-6-0s could run, and had plenty of power with 22in × 28in cylinders, and a well-tried type of boiler; their weakness was that steam pressure could not be reliably maintained. The Running Dept tried all the remedies; the chimney and blast pipe alignment was checked with a plumb-line, smokebox joints made airtight, tubes swept daily, and superheaters regularly water-tested for steam leakage. When Maunsell heard of the steaming difficulty, he had No 742 fitted with the cylinder indicating gear, and readings were taken on a run from Waterloo to Salisbury in February, 1924. In spite of expert handling the steam pressure gradually fell back until it was only 100lb at Hook: the highest indicated horse-power figure obtained was 950, with the pressure standing at 150lb, and at Hook it was as low as 650ihp. A month later, No 742 took the road again after having the steam ports enlarged, and the exhaust release point set a little earlier to sharpen up the blast. These alterations proved ineffective, so the next step was to alter the design of the chimney and petticoat pipe. Urie's distinctive, slightly Gallic stove-pipe chimney on the N15s was made of small diameter, in the belief that the exhaust would escape with considerable velocity and carry smoke and steam above the level of the cab windows, a problem that was to become serious, as will be related.

The stovepipe chimney on No 742 was replaced by the larger diameter pattern as used on the H15 class. It was a nicely-proportioned chimney which, with minor alterations and the addition of a capuchon, was to look well on the Arthurs, Schools and Nelsons. The larger petticoat pipe used with the H15 chimney enabled the blastpipe cap to be enlarged from 5in to 5⅛in, and on the next trial run with No 742 the steaming was much more consistent and the horse-power was up, to 1,250ihp.

Maunsell had by then decided to rebuild Nos 448–457 into his own version of the N15 with 200lb boiler pressure, 20½in diameter cylinders, long lap 6$\frac{9}{16}$in travel valves and with his design of super-heater with 337sq ft of heating surface instead of 308 sq ft with Urie's superheater. The main steam pipes to the valve chests took a direct path, out of the smokebox sides. The air passages through the ash-pan dampers to the grate were more generous than on the Urie N15. On test, No 451 proved capable of sustaining 1,500 indicated horse-power at 190lb pressure, a 20% improvement over No 742.

In the course of general repairs during 1927–29, the Urie N15s were given replacement Maunsell superheaters, and the worn 22in diameter cylinders were linered down to 20½in, except for No 755 which continued to run with the larger diameter without any appreciable advantage. As Nos 736–755 were to survive for forty-odd years, it was a pity that apart from the foregoing alterations they were left alone when they could have been placed on a par with the Maunsell version. The reason was that they satisfactorily filled a niche in the pattern of traffic requirements, coping with Southampton boat traffic, van trains and semi-fast passenger trains; it was thus difficult for the Running Dept to prove that further expenditure on them could be justified. In the mid-1930s, when new design work was practically at a standstill, the technical staff applied their minds to various ways of gingering up the Urie N15s. One simple method would have been to increase the boiler pressure from 180 to 200lb, but the works people were able to prove that the boiler repair costs of the Arthurs with 200lb pressure were appreciably greater than the 180lb boilers. It had been found necessary to have a number of spare 200lb boilers on hand, without which the target overhaul time for an Arthur could not be maintained.

An improvement in the valve events offered possibilities, and Nos 740/3/5/6/8/52 were equipped with double-ported valves which should have afforded better steam admission and a more free exhaust. Their effect on performance was very small. Better results followed the fitting of Nos 736/7/41/52/55 with Bulleid's arrangement of the multiple-jet blastpipe and big chimney.

Reverting to our story; when the storm broke in 1924 and it became imperative to supply some new passenger locomotives at once, without waiting for Maunsell's four-cylinder 4-6-0 design, the obvious course lay in taking the improved N15 design prepared for rebuilding Nos 448–457 to the Western section loading gauge, and altering details, such as the cab, to suit the composite loading gauge. This was to provide an N15 type 4-6-0 which could run on the Central section and on the Eastern section when the main-line to Dover via Tonbridge had been improved by the Civil Engineer to carry locomotives with axle-loads of 20 tons. The 30 additional locomotives which were decided upon, could not be built immediately at Eastleigh Works, and an urgent contract was undertaken by the North British Locomotive Company of Glasgow. Known in the trade as The Combine, the NB Co was the largest locomotive building firm in Europe, formed by the amalgamation of three former Glasgow firms, Sharp, Stewart & Co, Neilson, Reid & Co, and Dubs & Co, and the three workshops, Queens Park, Hyde Park and Atlas Works had a potential output of 700 locomotives per year. Delivery of the series No 763–792 began in May, 1925, barely six months after the placing of the Southern's order.

The locomotives, fully erected except for coupling and connecting rods, were towed from Glasgow to Eastleigh. Some ran hot on the journey, with overheated coupled axlebox bearings, which the contractors had made too neat a fit and with insufficient working clearance. By July, enough of them were serviceable to take over the Dover boat trains, of 425 tons instead of 300 tons.

It was at that time that the N15s began to appear with names. The circumstances in which the names came to be bestowed on them have been related by Sir John Elliot who was later to become Chairman of British Railways, and of London Transport. As Mr Elliot he wrote: I was at the time, 1925, Public Relations Assistant to Sir Herbert Walker. One day he sent for me and told me that a large number of new express engines were to be built at Eastleigh and Glasgow, and that he would like some special publicity given to them, suggesting that if I could find an appropriate name for them, he would recommend it to the Board of Directors. After a few days I submitted a list of the names of Arthur's Knights of the Round Table, pointing out the connection between them and places on the Southern Railway.'

Certainly, the romantic and dignified names were most suitable for locomotives, the most human of machines; more suitable, one might suggest, than the names of places. Many a parent, dragged to the end of the platform before starting time by a youngster eager to see the engine, 'Dad', must have been taxed with questions about

King Arthur or, more difficult still, about such Norman–French names as *Sir Meliot de Logres*.

It is fairly well-established that Arthur did exist, though he was a duke rather than a king, and that about 500AD he was the leader of the Britons against the Anglo-Saxons who invaded the country during the years following the departure of the Romans. He succeeded for a time in holding back the barbarian invaders, to preserve the orderly and peaceful existence which Britons had enjoyed under Roman rule, and his exploits were handed down by myths and legends. William of Malmesbury, in the 12th century, referring to the fables about Arthur, described him as 'a man worthy to be celebrated not by idle fictions but by authentic history. He long upheld the sinking state and roused the broken spirit of his country-men to war'. Nennins, writing in the 9th century, mentioned twelve battles in which Arthur was victorious but the British place names cannot be identified. Geoffrey of Monmouth, another 12th century writer, produced an historical romance, *The History of the Kings of Britain*, containing stories of Arthur; the book in due course inspired Sir Thomas Malory in the 15th century to write the dreamland tales in his *Morte d'Arthur*. More recently, Alfred, Lord Tennyson's 19th-century poem, *The Idylls of the King*, presented King Arthur as an ideal hero of English chivalry.

The connection between King Arthur and places in Southern Railway territory, such as Canterbury, Winchester, Old Sarum (Salisbury), Glastonbury, Camelford and Tintagel was, therefore, based on mediaeval legends. That these places were associated with the stirring events of the 5th and 6th centuries AD, historians accept as not entirely fanciful.

Fourteen more Arthurs, Nos 793–806, were built at Eastleigh between March, 1926 and January, 1927 to work on the Central section. The Baltics could handle the 'Brighton Belle' and other primary services to the coast, but with only seven of them in total and seldom all serviceable, they were being helped out by the River class 2-6-4 tanks, those much-lamented engines, well-liked by drivers in spite of a tendency to roll. Their riding was, in fact, much steadier on the Central than on the Eastern section. Experiments to improve it were cut short by the Sevenoaks accident. Some Drum-mond L12 4-4-0s, 'Bulldogs', were also at work on such trains as the 'Eastbourne Sunday Pullman'.

The last batch of Arthurs were provided with six-wheel tenders because the Civil Engineer considered the bogie tender, weighing 57½ tons—with more than 22 tons of water!—to be too heavy for the

Central, and certainly the mileages involved did not warrant the provision of so much water. A stock Ashford pattern of six-wheel tender was used, to suit which the drag-box of the Arthur had to be specially adapted, so that the 793–806 batch could not easily be changed to bogie tenders. The electrification to Brighton on the dc system was not expected to displace them as early as 1933 but they were quite suitable for the Kent Coast trains.

The SR Board had authorised the construction of fifteen Arthurs to follow No 792, but No 807 was not built and the number remained blank; instead the 15th became No 850 *Lord Nelson*, described in the next chapter.

The Arthurs were the first locomotives in Great Britain to be fitted with smokebox 'wings', or deflector plates, and their introduction to British practice came about in the following way. In 1902 the LSWR began the installation of pneumatically-operated points and signals on the main-line, first at Grateley and later over the 24 miles between Woking and Basingstoke. On the latter, four-track section the signals, carried on gantries, were placed immediately over each track with the object of indicating clearly to which line they applied. With the signals so placed, there was one snag: the driver's line of sight could be interrupted by the steam and smoke from the chimney. A much better arrangement, adopted when the Southern Railway installed colour-light signalling between Waterloo and Hampton Court Junction, was to place each signal slightly to the left of the track to which it applied. With left-hand drive engines—the majority—if a driver wanted to make certain of his correct signal he had, to quote Col Hall, the SR Signal Engineer of the time, 'only to cock his head over the side of the cab to see the right one'.

As locomotive boilers grew in size and chimneys got shorter, so the difficulties of sighting signals increased, and with more efficient valve gears the exhaust steam left the chimney at less velocity, with a tendency to drift down over the cab windows. Such a tendency was more pronounced with head or following winds than with cross winds. On the Woking–Basingstoke stretch the prevailing winds, south-westerly in Britain, blew in the same direction as the track. Another main-line likely to be similarly affected was the GWR West of England line, but that company placed its signals away from the centre of the track, and its locomotives had taper boilers and a width of cab which took advantage of a generous loading gauge.

By 1925, the improvements incorporated in the Maunsell Arthurs, which have previously been described, made signal sighting from these engines even more tricky, and drivers on the Western section petitioned Maunsell for a remedy. He, as was his wont, cast around to see whether other railway administrations were seriously troubled, and found that the German Railways obtained good results by fitting large rectangular plates vertically each side of the smokebox. Plates of this pattern were fitted to No 772 *Sir Percivale* working on the Western section in 1926. Though effective, they seemed a somewhat clumsy solution, so experiments were made to see whether small wings around the chimney would give the same results. They did not. A further alternative was tried, with a circular plate extending around the upper half of the smokebox, but this, too, failed. Maunsell then reverted to the German pattern but reduced in size: satisfactory results were achieved with plates as high as the handrails, well radiused on the top front corners. With these compromises the Arthurs and Nelsons were permanently fitted. Thus far, a solution had been reached by trial and error; in 1931, scale models of a Schools class and a U class with taper boiler were submitted for wind-tunnel tests at the National Physical Laboratory, and various patterns of deflector-plate were tested in miniature. One pattern extended the whole length of the engine from smokebox to cab. It was established that the projection of the plates forward of the smokebox provided the necessary up-draught to carry smoke clear of the boiler top. Without them, the air disturbance caused by the front of the smokebox gave rise to areas of low pressure around the boiler. Deflector plates were also adopted for certain LMS and LNER locomotives, but the GWR found no need of them.

The SR enginemen were pleased with the improved visibility, and soon discovered another advantage of deflector plates: pheasants and partridges that flew into the path of the engine were neatly trapped and ready for collection at the next stopping place!

No 783 *Sir Gillemore* fitted with experimental smoke deflectors./
H. C. Casserley

Three missing bolts and this loose deflector plate of an 'Arthur'
ripped the door-handles from a passing train./*Author*

An Arthur unusually piloted by a Drummond T9 No 117 on a down West of England train at Templecombe./*Author*

No 782 *Sir Brian* on Kent coast train with SECR stock./*P. Ransome-Wallis*

No 788 *Sir Urre of the Mount* on down Weymouth train. A LSWR
coach can be seen next to the engine.

No 769 *Sir Balan* at Petts Wood on down boat train./*E. R.
Wethersett*

No 457 *Sir Bedivere* emerges from Honiton Tunnel on down
Exeter train./*H. C. Casserley*

No 448 *Sir Tristram* and a Drummond K10. 4-4-0 at Salisbury./*LPC*

Above : No 457 *Sir Bedivere* on a wet evening at Waterloo, carrying
West of England headlamp code./*Topical Press*

Below : No 806 *Sir Galleron* on the turntable at Victoria.

Foot : No 797 *Sir Blamor de Gamis* at Cannon Street alongside
L class No 1760./*H. M. Madgwick*

Left: The footplate of an Arthur./*BR*

Above: The footplate of a Nelson./*BR*

The boiler of a Nelson./*BR*

No 850 *Lord Nelson* new at Eastleigh, 1926./*BR*

The Design of the Nelsons

In 1915 the story went round railway engineers' offices that some 4-6-0 locomotives had been built by Hawthorn, Leslie & Co of Newcastle for the Highland Railway, only to be debarred by the company's Civil Engineer; in consequence the Locomotive Superintendent who designed and ordered them had either been dismissed or compelled to resign. The locomotives had subsequently been bought by the Caledonian Railway. The full circumstances were not made public but for some reason there had been a lack of liaison between the officers concerned about the maximum axle-load that the Highland's track and bridges could safely bear.

The affair served as a reminder, where such was necessary, that locomotives were necessarily growing in size and weight, and that the margin of safety incorporated in the design of bridges built many years previously was gradually being reduced. The time was approaching when some bridges would be seriously overstressed, with the possible repetition of earlier disasters. Cast iron components were prone to fail without any warning; bridges of rivetted, wrought iron had the advantage that signs of distress, such as buckled plates and broken rivets, could afford some warning of trouble. Stresses increased with train speeds, but the extent of the stressing which was taking place was unknown, until the arrival of the electrical strain gauge made accurate measurement possible. It had been a broken cast-iron bridge girder that caused a serious derailment on the LBSCR at Norwood in May 1891; the locomotive involved was an 0-4-2 of the B1 class, No 175 *Hayling*.

In 1923 a Bridge Stress Committee, consisting of ten eminent civil engineers, was formed to investigate the problem. Five years later its report was published, and one of its points was that three- and four-cylinder locomotives, by virtue of better balancing than two-cylinder types, were much to be preferred.

It was during the same period that Maunsell was developing his design for a locomotive capable of running over all the Southern main-lines with trains of 500 tons at 55mph average speed. The SR limit of axle-loading was 21 tons, and the weight on the King Arthur driving axle was already within 16cwts of the limit at 20 tons 4cwt.

45

No easement of the limit was likely; the Southern Chief Civil Engineer, George Ellson, was a member of the Bridge Stress Committee and, as a former engineer on the SECR, he knew that some bridge reconstruction work was necessary, before even the Arthurs could pass over the Eastern section routes.

The Lord Nelson design deserves a special place in the history of British locomotive development, as an exercise in ingenuity to secure a significant increase in the power of a 4-6-0 type with a minimal increase in weight. As it turned out, the empty weight of a Nelson engine at 77 tons 2cwt was only 1 ton 1cwt greater than an Arthur of the final 793–806 series, and yet the tractive effort was raised to 33,510lb against the 25,321lb of the Arthur. The weight, in working order, on each coupled axle of the original Nelson was 20 tons 13cwt compared with 20 tons 4cwt on the driving axle of the Arthur, and after the Nelsons had been given new cylinders and a re-designed front-end by Mr Bulleid, the axle weights were still within the 21-ton limit.

In view of the findings of the Bridge Stress Committee, it was to be expected that thereafter Maunsell's proposals for express locomotives were multi-cylinder types: the three-cylinder Schools class 4-4-0 which followed the Nelsons, and the three-cylinder 2-6-2 and four-cylinder 4-6-2, neither of which got beyond the drawing board. Some reduction in the hammer-blow of the two-cylinder Arthurs was achieved meanwhile, by re-calculating the proportion of balancing weights for the reciprocating parts. Subsequently the correct balance of driving wheels was checked by spinning them in the special machine at Eastleigh.

In working out the Nelson design, considerable time was spent on a complete investigation into the problems of balancing reciprocating masses, and the arrangement of setting the cranks at 135 degrees to give eight beats or 'impulses' per revolution of the coupled wheels offered advantages in the reduction of stress on axleboxes and motion parts. Holcroft had pointed this out in a paper read in 1920. The latter were made out of the latest high-tensile steel and the working parts of the Lord Nelson were a model of neatness combined with strength. In order to test the eight-beat principle beforehand, a Drummond four-cylinder, No 449, was altered to that crank arrangement in 1924. It created a more even draught on the fire and there was less tendency for the blast to pull the fire to pieces when the engine was working heavily at slow speed. On the other hand, it was argued that the blast would be too soft to be fully effective, and that four impulses instead of eight would be better for starting heavy trains. The trial proved that the strength was quite adequate. Some years later the last of the class, No 865, *Sir John Hawkins*, had the crank settings altered to four beats, to enable direct comparisons to be made between it and the others. After a long period it was clear that there was no difference. Some drivers declared in favour of No 865, others opined that the 'bark' had improved, but not the 'bite'. The alteration to the engine was one of several experiments with others of the class, of which more anon.

The only British locomotive on which the eight-beat crank setting had been tried was a four-cylinder 0-6-0 tank engine produced in 1922 by the North Staffordshire Railway. The intention there was to improve the acceleration of suburban trains, but the engine was unsuccessful. After *Lord Nelson* had appeared, five LMS Claughtons were fitted with Caprotti valve gear and eight-beat cranks, and the Crown Agents utilised the same setting in some Pacifics built by Vulcan Foundry for the then North-Western Railway, India (later Pakistan Railways).

The Nelson boiler was based on that of the Maunsell N class 2-6-0 boiler, enlarged to the limit of the composite loading gauge. The grate area of 33sq ft was the largest of any British 4-6-0, except the GWR King class of 1927; to achieve it the firebox was 10ft 6in long and although it was only 18in longer than the King Arthur firebox the extra distance of the front firebars from the firehole required a lot more skill in the use of the shovel. If the fireman was unable to shoot shovelfuls of coal to the far front of the box two things happened: the unfed areas of grate would burn thin and large volumes of cold air would be drawn in, and coal which fell short of its intended place would form a high ridge across the middle of the grate, to add further to the difficulty of hitting the front. The result was a rapid fall in steam pressure; meanwhile the fireman endeavoured, with the aid of a long fire-iron not easily manipulated when travelling at speed, to spread the fuel more evenly over the grate. Stirring the fire was, on any locomotive, liable to lead to the condition described as 'having 100lb of smoke and no steam'. The Nelson boiler steamed freely in the hands of a fireman who had mastered it, but disappointing runs were to be expected otherwise. For this reason the Nelsons were allocated during their lifetime to only four depots—Nine Elms and Stewarts Lane up to 1939, and later to Eastleigh and Bournemouth, and so far as possible kept out of the hands of enginemen who did not get regular practice with them.

The copper firebox tubeplate and the steel throat plate, at the junction of firebox and boiler barrel, were elaborate pressings with pronounced ogee curves, and the tube-holes in the firebox plate came close to the radii at the root of the flanges. Evidence of stress in these portions of the boiler took the form of cracks, and leakages from the tube seatings, stresses which were aggravated by allowing an engine to stand with the blower on, dampers and firedoor open and the grate not fully covered. Attention from running shed boiler-smiths accounted for rather frequent days out of steam and out of service, but the position improved after minor improvements and when the three-roller tube expander was replaced by the five-roller, less likely to distort the tube holes.

With competent firing, and careful boiler maintenance, the Nelson was a first-class locomotive, capable of keeping the faster schedules with ease. The four separate sets of Walschaerts valve gear gave accurate beats; the good balancing obviated any feeling of riding on a reciprocating engine, and the regular drivers and fire-men became very attached to them. But as it turned out, the 500-ton trains for which they were intended were few; the regular ones were those made up of Wagon-Lits stock for the 'Night Ferry', and 'Golden Arrow' and 'Bournemouth Belle' which loaded to twelve Pullmans in the summer. A 500-ton train of ordinary SR stock involved fourteen coaches and a dining-car, and only one platform at Water-loo could accommodate a train of that length. For the regular-interval expresses twelve coaches were normally sufficient and within the capacity of the Arthurs. Hence it came about that much of the mileage run by Nelsons could have been performed by a less powerful type, and at less cost per mile, as a Nelson consumed more coal with its larger grate, and more oil with four cylinders, and was more expensive to overhaul than the two-cylinder Arthur. History does not relate the basis on which the operating department calcul-ated the need for sixteen Nelsons, in 1928, but traffic forecasts had reason to be optimistic, and having passed through a period of acute shortage, the management was anxious to have more reserves of motive power.

With a boiler pressure of 220lb, cylinder 16½in diam and 6ft 7in diameter coupled wheels, the tractive effort of *Lord Nelson* exceeded that of the GWR Castle class. The publicity people at Paddington had made much of the claim that the Castle was the most powerful express passenger engine in the country and when *Lord Nelson* ousted it from that position, the publicity from Waterloo was not slow in pointing this out, though it was hardly likely to produce a rush of passengers eager to travel to the West of England by the SR route instead of the GWR! It was much to Maunsell's distaste, since the CME staff at Swindon had been most co-operative in supplying information (about design problems of four-cylinder locomotives) while the Nelson was in embryo stage. Collaboration was much to be preferred to pointless rivalry.

No 850 *Lord Nelson* left Eastleigh Works in August 1926, with the flourish of press trumpets that befitted 'the premier express locomotive in the British Isles'. In those days a new locomotive aroused interest everywhere it went. Maunsell was pleased and honoured when King George VI and Queen Elizabeth the Queen Mother (then Duke and Duchess of York) took a short footplate trip on No 850 in the course of a visit to Ashford Works on October 21st, 1926—appropriately, Trafalgar Day.

Two years elapsed before any more Nelsons were built. No 850 underwent a series of coal consumption trials on booked services; no special runs were made and no dynamometer car was used. Maunsell was determined to discover, and to put right, any faults in the first engine, rather than build a number and be faced with the expense of alterations to the batch. During the initial trial period, No 850 worked all the principal trains on the Eastern and Western sections without difficulty. On the trip customarily given for the benefit of the press, a twelve-coach train was taken easily at the 55mph average from Waterloo to Salisbury. On July 27th, 1927, the 10.45am Victoria–Dover boat train, carrying the King of Egypt and his suite, was the heaviest single-engined train to have been worked out of Victoria, extra Pullmans for the royal party having made the load up to 480 tons full.

Thus assured that the engine was reliable, that the boiler steamed freely and that the coal, oil and water consumption figures were reasonable, Maunsell could confidently proceed with the building of a further fifteen engines, Nos 851–865, in 1928. Meantime, *Lord Nelson* had bowed to *King George V* for the top place in the power rating of British locomotives. The GW King class was, however, heavier. A review of the bridges on the GWR brought to light the fact that, on the routes where a heavier and more powerful locomotive than the Castle class could be employed with advantage, an axle-load of $22\frac{1}{2}$ tons was permissible; also that bridges built by the GWR since 1900 had been designed for axle-loads up to that figure—a far-sighted precaution.

With Chatham, Portsmouth and Plymouth dockyards and other Naval bases on its system, the Southern was prompted to use the names of famous Admirals and the gunmetal plates which bore them were applied in style; no mere surnames on oblong plates but with massive, curved plates. The longer ones took two men to lift them: no weight-saving there!

The Nelsons, as new, were hand-painted by the traditional methods, being taken to a warmed paint shop and given numerous coats of flat, undercoat and gloss, well rubbed down. The Southern, after deliberating as to which of the passenger locomotive liveries used by the constituent companies looked the most presentable after two or three years of weathering, came down in favour of the green used on the LSWR and introduced by Urie in 1913. This was described as sage green, and known in the paint shop as Parsons Green—not a reference to a London suburb nor to the colour of the vicar's lawn, but to the name of the manufacturer. The colour was subject to slight changes in shade as years went on. Lining was in chrome yellow. Brass number plates were fitted to the cab sides. The appearance of the finished locomotive—without the ugly deflector plates—could appropriately be termed 'ship-shape' meaning, according to the Universal English Dictionary, 'arranged as a good seaman would approve of'. In 1927 the Royal Scot 4-6-0s of the LMS appeared, with a distinct likeness to the Lord Nelson, the result of friendly collaboration between Derby and Waterloo. The three-cylinder Royal Scot proved to be the better of the two. The boiler was almost a copy of the Nelson boiler but had a slope and depth of grate that was easier to fire and the chimney and blastpipe dimensions turned out to be correct for good draughting and steaming, more by fortunate choice than from any testing data available.

Their shorter engine wheelbase gave the Scots a steadiness of ride inferior to the Nelsons. In December, 1929 the leading coupled wheels of a Nelson working an up boat train became derailed at Kent House, and after damaging a short length of track the wheels rerailed themselves and the train arrived at Victoria with the driver blissfully unaware of what had happened. That kind of off-and-on again derailment was not unknown with freight wagons but very rare with locomotives. By an odd coincidence, a Royal Scot did the same thing at Weaver Junction a few weeks afterwards. The occurrences naturally raised the question as to the extent to which the bogie and the leading coupled wheels 'steered' a locomotive on curves, and led to a review of the design of bogie side-control springs.

The Scots also suffered from drifting steam, and Derby tried at least four versions of mini-deflectors, just as the Southern had done, before adopting the large deflectors already applied to Arthurs and Nelsons. Incidentally, Doncaster also spent much time with devices of its own before deciding that, after all, Maunsell had been right.

Modifications to the Nelsons

Various engines of the Nelson class were subjected to modification by Maunsell, not because improvements were by any means essential but because Maunsell was not wedded to theories and preferred to confirm them, or otherwise, by practical applications. It had long been a theory that smaller-diameter driving wheels were necessary on heavily-graded sections, as compared with easier routes, and in Drummond's time on the LSWR locomotives intended for working west of Salisbury were given 6ft diameter driving wheels instead of those of 6ft 7in in general use elsewhere on that system. In practice, the larger diameter wheel displayed no disadvantage, and, on a switchback route, was an advantage on the downhill and level stretches.

In Maunsell's tentative design for a 2-6-2 passenger locomotive a 6ft 3in wheel was proposed, and to clinch the argument about driving-wheel sizes, Nelson No 859 *Lord Hood* was fitted with 6ft 3in driving wheels. The locomotive was tried both on the Eastern and the Western sections, including some running between Salisbury and Exeter, in direct comparison with sister engines, but not the slightest difference could be detected in performance.

Another theory put to the test was in regard to the length of boiler tubes. The length of the boiler barrel of the standard Nelson boiler had been decided by the length of tubes, 13ft 9in, stocked at Eastleigh for N15 and H15 boilers, although a longer barrel could have been used and the additional weight would have been borne by the bogie, and would not have increased the coupled-axle weights. In theory, longer tubes would extract more heat from the flue-gases, and help to raise the temperature of the feed water which fed through clack-boxes on the front ring of the boiler barrel. Someone suggested to Maunsell that adherence to a common tube length had been a case of penny-wise pound-foolish on the part of Eastleigh drawing office, so when the eleventh engine, No 860 *Lord Hawke*, was built, the boiler barrel was increased by 10in. Again, the answer was a lemon; No 860 did not steam better than the others.

In theory, compound expansion increased the efficiency of the steam engine. Continental locomotive engineers had made a

A Nelson in final form; front-end altered by Bulleid.

A Schools as built in original condition. Smoke deflector plates were added later.

COAL 5 TONS

WATER 5000 GALLS

$3'5\frac{1}{2}''$

$3'7''$ DIA.

12'3'' 6'6'' 6'0'' 6'6'' 5'0''

ASE

28T. 6C. 28T. 8C.

G ORDER 141T. 9C 57T. 19C.

COAL 5 TONS

WATER 4000 GALLS

$3'5\frac{1}{2}''$

5'3'' 7'' $4'3\frac{1}{4}''$ $4'0''$ DIA 6'6'' 6'6'' $6'1\frac{3}{4}''$

$10'1\frac{1}{4}''$ 13'0''

OVERALL

13T. 17C 14T. 1C 14T. 10C

& TENDER IN WKG ORDER 109T.10C 42T 8C

practical success of it whereas British engineers had not, with the exception of the Smith-Deeley Midland Compound 4-4-0. The principle still intrigued designers in spite of the limitations upon cylinder diameters imposed by the British loading gauge. A compound had been proposed for the first LMS express locomotive, and in 1931 Maunsell seriously considered converting a Nelson, with two 15½in diameter high-pressure cylinders and two 22in low-pressure cylinders. It was to be fitted with a proprietary make of poppet valve gear, of which the LNER was making extensive trial. Both projects were dropped, probably because Maunsell realised that his department did not have the resources to carry out major development work.

In 1936, No 857 *Lord Howe* came out of Eastleigh Works with a new boiler which made the engine look longer and more massive than before. Within the round-topped boiler the front of the firebox projected forward into the barrel to form a combustion-chamber, a feature which, according to evidence from other railways, made for more complete combustion of the gaseous components of the coal. Maunsell's proposed Pacific was being planned, with the intention that it would carry such a boiler.

No 857 was tried out on Victoria–Dover boat trains; it steamed more freely than the standard boiler, except when the engine had to be driven hard; clearly, the draughting was wrong and further experiments were needed with the blastpipe and chimney. Dynamo-meter-car recordings of the vacuum in the smokebox, and at grate level, and analyses of the flue gases would have proved invaluable, if these could have been procured. For some reason, no further interest was taken in No 857, with Maunsell's retirement in the following year.

Experiments with a four-beat crank axle on No 865 *Sir John Hawkins* have already been mentioned. The first really noticeable improvement in performance was observed in 1934 when No 862 *Lord Collingwood* was fitted with a Kylchap blastpipe and chimney, the joint invention of Monsieur Kylala and Monsieur Chapelon of the SNCF. The device improved the draught significantly, at the same time reducing the back-pressure on the exhaust steam. Despite favourable reports from the Locomotive Running Department, this improvement was not followed up immediately.

In 1938, some of the Nelsons were fitted with recording speedo-meters, and examination of the paper rolls on which speeds were marked revealed quite a crop of 100mph bursts. By that time, Mr O. V. S. Bulleid had become CME and during his first eighteen months on the Southern he made numerous footplate trips. He was particularly interested in the Nelsons and made a series of memorable footplate appearances on the 'Golden Arrow'. He was convinced that the schedule between Victoria and Dover could be cut by higher speeds on rising gradients. On his instructions, No 862 *Lord Collingwood* was driven in full gear up Grosvenor Road bank out of Victoria, and then at 40–50% cut-off for the rest of the journey. Along the straight between Tonbridge and Ashford, with wide-open regulator and both injectors working to keep the boiler water level in sight in the water-gauges, speeds were between 90 and 95mph. By the time he reached Dover the fireman, appropriately named Bull, was pretty well exhausted, but Bulleid was delighted. As Gresley's assistant on the LNER he had been on some hair-raising runs with the streamlined A4 Pacifics, and had accompanied the LNER 2-8-2 *Cock o' the North* to the SNCF testing plant at Vitry. His experience of improved front-end design led him to have the Nelsons fitted with Lemaitre five-jet multiple blastpipes during 1938/39. Although a particularly clumsy chimney accompanied the modification, it clearly improved their performance. At the same time, he ordered Eastleigh to design new cylinders with 10in diam piston valves instead of 8in diam, and with improved steam and exhaust passages. Seven locos were so fitted in 1939–40, Nos 852/5/6/7/60/2/5. With the exception of Nos 851 and 863, which retained their original cylinders, the remainder were re-cylindered when renewal was necessary during overhaul. To cap this final modification, Nos 851 and 863 were none the worse without it!

A propos the straight, almost level 26 miles between Tonbridge and Ashford, a regular Nelson driver who had been a young fireman in SECR days recalled the *joie de vivre* engendered by the effortless speeds which even the old Stirling engines could maintain there. The little wayside stations along the Weald were illuminated at night by oil lamps fixed to the platform fence, at about footplate height. The passage of a fast train was liable to blow them out, and the extinguishing draught could be increased by the fireman's leaning out with a firing shovel to act as a fan. After passing a station in this fashion, he and his driver would look back, to count the nightly 'score'. At other times, coal would be piled on the fire to create as much smoke as possible; the boat train would be enveloped in a thick, black cloud, whereupon the driver would chuckle: "They'll think they're on the boat already, make it thicker and they'll think it's a bloomin' liner."

The Nelsons started life with the Urie pattern of double-bogie tender. This was Urie's improved version of the eight-wheel Drummond 'water-cart'; it did not leak nor melt its bearings. It was not, however, self-trimming although the fireman could easily climb back into the coal space as the footplate end was virtually open apart from a low partition fitted with a guillotine pattern of coal door. Two simple toolboxes were provided in each front corner. The final version designed just prior to World War II had a sharper slope to the bunker floor to induce the coal to tumble forwards, and the sides were raised to increase the depth of the bunker. The capacity of 5 tons of coal and 5,000 gallons of water remained the same as earlier tenders. At the footplate end, vertical cupboards, including a 'clean one for clothes', provided a draught and dust screen. In Maunsell's time, there was some swapping of various patterns of bogie tenders, partly in connection with the Maunsell S15 4-6-0 freight locos, and the provision of tenders for the N15x rebuilt LBSCR Baltics.

It must be mentioned that the tender was not only a vehicle for coal and water: it provided considerable braking power and carried vacuum reservoirs. When working loose-coupled freight trains down long falling gradients, a big bogie tender played an important part in controlling the train. The hand-brake could be screwed on and left on for many miles without overheating the wheels and brake-blocks, with the engine brake in reserve to stop the train. A tender had other uses. The stocks of stores at the locomotive depots were supplied by regular stores vans, but items required more quickly were transported on tenders. Large objects such as connecting and coupling rods were loaded on the flat space over the back part of the tender, and small parcels were carried in the tool-boxes. By this method, stocks of parts could be kept at the largest depots, and a part wanted by a smaller depot could be put on the next engine going in that direction. There were other consignments of a less official and more perishable nature: Devonshire cream, fresh fish from Folkestone or Padstow, turkeys at Christmas. They might well bear the official printed label marked OCS—On Company's Service—which could also be translated as 'Old Cadger's Society'. In the days when Nine Elms men working the overnight goods to Weymouth lodged at Dorchester, so the story went, a live pig bought in Dorchester market found its way back to London on the back of a tender, and survived!

The Design of the Schools

When the civil engineers had completed, in 1852, a branch of the South Eastern Railway from Tunbridge Wells to St Leonards they could not have imagined what problems they had created for future generations, by their having chosen to construct it to a loading gauge even more restricted than that of the owning company's other lines. In due course, thousands of freight vehicles were to carry an inscription that they were not allowed between Tonbridge and Hastings and the owning company was building passenger stock specially for the line, six inches narrower in width than the normal coaches. Railway companies all over the country carried, in their Appendixes to the Working Timetables, details of the limited dimensions of vehicles which could be allowed, with the added warning 'No vehicle with Guards' Side Observatories can be accepted for this branch'.

The small double-line tunnel at Mountfield near Battle was the major obstacle, and it became even smaller when the tunnel lining had to be reinforced by an extra layer of brickwork. The clearance between trains passing in the tunnel is so close that, on one occasion when an error occurred in the track alignment, at one point, the offside door handles were sheared off the two trains. A century after the opening of the line, various solutions were under serious consideration: enlargement of the tunnel, its even more costly conversion to a deep cutting or the installation of a specially controlled, single, reversible line. The problem remains to this day, in association with possible electrification.

The Southern Railway succeeded in making the former SECR main-lines suitable to carry Arthurs and Nelsons, but they were far too large for the Hastings route, over which traffic had reached a state when better motive power was needed. A locomotive was required which would be powerful enough to haul the Charing Cross–Hastings trains to the same timings between London and Tonbridge as the Kent coast trains hauled by the Arthurs, ie of similar tractive effort.

When the proposition came under consideration in 1928 it was evident, in the first place, that to conform to the maximum permitted width, 8ft 6½in, over the Hastings line, an engine with two outside cylinders large enough to provide sufficient power was out of the question: the width over the cylinders would be too great. A two-cylinder engine, whether outside or inside cylinders, would not be acceptable to the civil engineer with an axle-load of 21 tons; if adopted, it would have to have a lesser axle-load on the coupled wheels to allow for the two-cylinder hammer-blow, on which the Bridge Stress Committee had commented adversely. There would also be less weight for adhesion, and there was not much level line between Charing Cross and Hastings. Clearly, a multi-cylinder engine was the answer, and three cylinders of 16½in diameter—the same as the Nelsons—could be fitted within a width of 8ft 5 7/16 in.

For adhesion a six-coupled design, and nothing less, would have been the obvious choice, had it not been for the Hastings line. A shorter frame would have less throw-over on curves and thus more easily kept within the restriction on width, and a four-coupled engine would be more suitable for the sharp curves between Tonbridge and Hastings. Added to which, the four-coupled engine was cheaper to build and maintain; its internal resistance was lower (ie more free-running than a six-coupled) and less power was spent in propelling itself owing to its lighter weight. These advantages were to be amply demonstrated later, when the Schools class proved such a success everywhere. Finally, a four-coupled engine suited the existing turntables—a lesser consideration, perhaps; nevertheless, a new turntable cost as much as a new locomotive. A Schools could turn on a 50ft diameter table; Arthurs and Nelsons required 60ft and 65ft tables respectively.

Taking everything into account, the decision was made in favour of a four-coupled, three-cylinder engine with 6ft 7in wheels and a boiler pressure of 220lb. The tractive effort at 85% boiler pressure worked out at 25,130 lb: almost the same as an Arthur but weighing the equivalent of one coach less. With 21 tons on each coupled axle—the power to weight ratio was 598lb/ton. This was a high ratio and close to the limit desirable to avoid excessive proneness to wheel-slip. The Schools were to need careful handling to avoid it.

In order to simplify construction and the provision of spares, much of the new design was identical with the Nelsons: the wheel sizes, the outside cylinders, the motion parts and many other details. Even the front cab windows were the same, turned upside-down to suit! When it came to the boiler, the Nelson pattern could not be followed. To conform to the Hastings gauge the cab had to be reduced in width over the cornices and therefore the upper cab sides had to be canted inwards. A cab of this shape dictated a round-topped firebox rather than a Belpaire type, which would also have made the boiler too heavy. The boiler was virtually an Arthur boiler reduced in length. The grate area was ample with 28·3sq ft; the 8ft 3½in length of grate was easy to fire. The short boiler barrel—2ft less than the Arthur—affected the length of the superheater tubes with the result that the superheat temperature was lower than the optimum by current standards. In all other respects, the boiler pressure, the valve gear, the steam pipe and port areas and the balancing, the Schools design could hardly have been better if it had been concocted twenty-five years later. The multiple-jet blastpipe was the one later development and was fitted to eighteen engines.

The tenders carried 4,000 gallons of water and 5 tons of coal on six wheels. From No 910 onwards they were made more comfortable by arranging a bank of tool and clothes lockers across the footplate, which also gave better weather protection. Even better in this respect was a tender, fitted to No 932, on which the sides were raised at the footplate end to match the cab sides. Similar improvement was made to all the Nelson tenders.

For the new 4-4-0s, officially Class V in the SR alphabetical classification, names were sought which would be a change from the sort of subjects already covered by named locomotives in the country, and preferably having some connection with the Southern. Considerable business was done in school traffic; there were numerous public and private boarding schools in the South, which at the beginning and end of term chartered special trains, or coaches attached to ordinary trains, to and from London. Consequently, the names for the engines were of well-known public schools, but rather than confine the list to those on the Southern system, which could have involved some invidious preferences, those chosen were a representative selection of schools both south and north of the Thames. Wherever possible, a new engine was taken to the station near the school for exhibition to the boys. A press photograph of one such occasion showed boys clambering all over the engine; a couple of them polishing the nameplate provided the caption 'Keep the name bright'.

The first engine left Eastleigh in March 1930. A batch of ten had been ordered to cover the London–Hastings service but as it happened the Civil Engineer required more time to bring the Tonbridge-St Leonards section up to standard and permission for the Schools to use the line was withheld until the following year, 1931. This proved fortunate as the ten engines were completed and put into service during 1930, and had the opportunity of showing their paces on the Eastern and Western section main-lines, with some startling results. No 909 *St Paul's*, for example, on an ordinary run from Salisbury to Waterloo, took 12 coaches weighing 420 tons full, over the 83.8 miles in a net time of 93¾ minutes. The climb to Grateley, 11 miles, took 20min 20sec; Worthing Junction, 33½ miles, was passed in 44min 52sec, and Surbiton, 71.8 miles, in 78min 45sec. The average speed from Worthing Junction to Surbiton was over 68mph. From a 4-4-0, this was great stuff, and soon every engineman was keen to try out a Schools.

On the Dover and Ramsgate route, they began to work the 80-min Folkestone Flyers, in place of the L1 4-4-0s. Along the straight between Tonbridge and Ashford, the Schools could cover the 26.4 miles in under 19 minutes with nine coaches.

On that fast length there were pronounced dips in the track beneath the overbridges, As has already been mentioned, when the South Eastern Railway was built, the depth between the formation and the sleepers allowed for a layer of ballast which was in time to prove quite inadequate for the traffic. Unless the formation was to be excavated at great cost, increasing the depth of ballast involved a rise in track level except where fixed structures such as overbridges limited the permissible alteration in rail height, hence the dips. At these places, the Schools were prone to bounce quite alarmingly owing to their short wheelbase and a centre of gravity near the middle (the driving) axle. The bogie axleboxes were actually striking both top and bottom stops when bouncing occurred, the movement being described as not unlike the contemporary Austin Seven crossing a hump-backed bridge! The trouble was overcome by fitting stiffer coil springs to the bogie axleboxes.

It was because of the restricted clearances on the Eastern section that an enamel notice-plate was fitted in the cabs of all Maunsell engines, warning drivers to take great care when leaning out. The coaches, too, had notices over the windows to the same effect, with wording in French *Ne se pencher au de hors.*

Ere long, the new engines were being described as 'the finest the Southern had ever built', a phrase which recurs in the recollections of retired staff. They were right, from the word go, and ten of them were put into service without any need to return to workshops for modifications. Later, during overhauls, the gravity sanding was replaced by steam sanding, partly to improve the adhesion and partly because at slow speed the gravity system supplied so much sand that it interfered with vital track circuits, particularly at

Top: Specially furbished and sent north for exhibition at the
Liverpool & Manchester Centenary celebrations in 1930, No 861
temporarily posed as No 850./*BR*

Above: A Nelson under construction./*BR*

Above: 'David and Goliath', 1927 version. *Lord Nelson*, alongside LBSCR No 214 *Gladstone* which had been purchased by the Stephenson Locomotive Society./*LPC*

Below: No 850 at Nine Elms fitted with indicator shelter.

Foot: No 850 on the 11am Victoria-Dover Marine. In 1929 the 11am became the 'Golden Arrow'./*F. R. Hebron*

No 859 *Lord Hood* leaving Shakespeare Cliff Tunnel with the down 'Golden Arrow' all-Pullman train, 1929.

No 850 leaves Waterloo with the 11am Waterloo-West of England on the inaugural run of the ACE. The old Waterloo 'A' signalbox is in the background./*Topical Press*

No 857 *Lord Howe* fitted with new boiler, 1936.

On the footplate of *Lord Howe,* belting along the Tonbridge-Ashford straight with a boat train./*Author*

Firing a Nelson, with careful aim and a watchful eye for thin places in the firebed./Author

No 862 Lord Collingwood fitted with Kylchap blastpipe and double chimney, at Herne Bay in 1937./P. Ransome-Wallis

Above: *Lord Howe* showing visible evidence of poor combustion.

Below: No 863 *Lord Rodney* fitted with new cylinders and Lemaitre blastpipe and chimney on a down boat train at Shortlands Junction in June 1939./*C. R. L. Coles*

Foot: Southampton, 1939. No 851 *Sir Francis Drake* with royal special, on the return of King George VI and Queen Elizabeth from their tour of North America./*Author*

"So you want to be a driver!" The side window of *Lord Nelson's* cab is of steel, not glass, as an air raid precaution in 1940./*Author*

No 2329 *Stephenson* in 1937—the Maunsell conversion of an
LBSCR Baltic./*BR*

The first Schools, No 900 *Eton* photographed in March 1930./*BR*

Waterloo, Charing Cross and Victoria where drivers of departing trains were inclined to be liberal with it.

The appeal of a Schools did not rest entirely on its ability to rival larger locomotives in performance. The number of successful 4-4-0s in existence testified to the popularity of the type in British practice: indeed, the 4-4-0 was regarded by many as being the optimum size of locomotive from a handling and servicing point of view. To take an analogy with the automobile world, for reasons not easy to define there are some in which a driver instinctively feels at one with his machine, and so it was with steam locomotives. A Schools was most pleasing to handle. The driver was well placed in relation to the front and rear buffers to judge the engine's position to a nicety when coupling up, and his view ahead did not suffer from the length of the boiler. With a quick-operating regulator a cautious and slip-free start could be made, waiting until the train was well on the move before giving the engine full steam. From that point the engine seemed to canter away with long strides, softly chittery-chattering at the chimney top and at the open firehole door. The originals with Maunsell chimney had no vulgar bark; almost as much noise was audible from the clank of the nickel-steel coupling and connecting rods.

Oddly enough, neither the Schools nor the Arthurs and Nelsons acquired nicknames, like 'Mongolipers' for Maunsell N class and 'Maggies' for the Z class. Drummond's T9 class 4-4-0s earned the name 'Greyhounds' for their free-running at speed, and certainly the Schools could have been similarly described.

The bracketing of some station names with those of adjacent schools indicated the importance to the railways of school traffic before the age of the motor car. The LBSCR had 'Christ's Hospital (West Horsham)', 'Shoreham for Lancing College' and 'North Dulwich for Dulwich College'. On the Somerset and Dorset Joint line there was 'Chilcompton for Downside', whilst on its Reading branch the SECR built 'Wellington College for Crowthorne'. On Southern territory there were more public schools than the forty Schools class engines and twenty-eight of them were included in the list. Apart from commencing with the most-publicised, Eton, the names were selected in no particular order, and after the first ten engines had been seen at work there were plenty of comments, and suggestions as to future naming! To make the choice less parochial and to minimise the risk of any ill-feeling that might follow the inevitable omissions of some Southern schools, Nos 919–930 were given the names of schools elsewhere. Amongst the names of the last nine engines were schools which qualified for precedence on grounds of age: indeed, King's School Canterbury (No 933) had its origins in the 7th century AD before Winchester, 1394, and Eton, 1440. Westminster, 1560, and Harrow, 1571, were two out of the many schools in the country which were founded in the 16th and 17th centuries, and it would have added interest if the engines had carried the names of the older schools only, with their foundation years shown on the nameplates, thus emphasising their historical significance in the growth of education.

During their last years, the Schools were used for Royal trains. On one such occasion, when the train was about to leave Victoria for Epsom Races, the following exchange of pleasantries was heard between the Duke of Edinburgh and the Southern's Superintendent of Operation:

> Prince Philip (leg-pulling): "Do you really think your engine will get there?"
> S.O.O.: "Sir, if Her Majesty's horse is half as good as our engine, it will come in first today!"

Train journeys by members of the Royal family and by eminent persons used to be more frequent than today, and Southern men were often privileged to be in attendance, on formal and informal occasions. Winston Churchill was always good for a friendly wave and, sometimes, for amusing repartee. One day when a small crowd had gathered to see him off by train (he was Prime Minister at the time) the clapping was marred by a rude 'boo'. 'Winnie' turned to face the interrupter and said with a chuckle, "Ah, I don't mind that noise a bit—after all, there are few countries left in the world where a man can say 'boo' to a head of state without being arrested!"

The Southern Workshops

Britain was the birthplace of the steam locomotive. As a heavy industry dependent upon ready supplies of iron, coal and steel, the principal locomotive building firms were to be found in the north, where smoke, noise and grey skies were part of the environment. In contrast, the locomotive, carriage and wagon workshops built by the predecessors of the Southern Railway were enviably situated; Ashford Works in a market town in Kent—the Garden of England— Brighton Works at a popular seaside resort, and Eastleigh on a rural site in the Itchen Valley. Lancing, an off-shoot of Brighton exclusively for carriages, was on the South coast. All three workshops had replaced the original ones in South London, at Battersea, New Cross and Nine Elms.

The most modern workshops when completed in 1911 were those at Eastleigh, on a site of 92 acres. With plenty of space available, the sections productive of dirt and fumes, the forges and the foundries, were housed separately from the erecting bays. Being away from the residential area the only people to be disturbed by the thumping of a 35-ton steam hammer and by the racket of pneumatic hammers in the boiler shop were the employees in the adjacent railway houses. The Schools, Nelsons and the Arthurs, except for the thirty built in Glasgow, were products of Eastleigh, in an era when rivetted construction had not given place to electric welding, untrustworthy as it was deemed, and when the use of oxy-gas for cutting metal was novel, as also was the use of motor trollies for carrying materials instead of a small army of labourers pushing wheelbarrows. Although the buildings were modern, most of the machine tools were elderly; one, an Armstrong-Whitworth screwing machine dated 1865, was in continuous use until 1935.

The time-honoured procedure for overhauling a locomotive was for it to be dismantled and then re-erected by one gang, the members of which took turns to accompany the trial run, ending up at some country station where it would be put into a siding to cool a warm axlebox, while the crew took refreshment in the local. After trial, the locomotive spent several weeks in the painting shop. This leisurely procedure was changed in 1931, following the lead of Crewe Works and its belt-system of rapid overhauls. Thereafter, each stage from stripping to re-erection was performed by specialist gangs, each confined to one routine operation and paint was applied in the erecting shop while assembly was taking place, regardless of foot-prints, finger-marks and dust. The change was not popular with the shops staff, but thereafter the complete overhaul of a King Arthur was reduced from three months to 19 days. Not that the locomotive was ready for work on the twentieth day, for it was likely to be shunted to the running shed minus floorboards, firebars and other parts.

It happened from time to time that a locomotive ex-works would, after return to its home depot, develop some fault, such as a loose cylinder or leaking boiler, for which the works was responsible. Such instances were liable to spark off an exchange of acrimonious correspondence between the respective head offices of the Loco-motive Running Department and the Chief Mechanical Engineer's Department; the latter, in keeping with the defensive attitude of railway departments generally, would express disbelief or a counter-accusation of maltreatment by the drivers and depot staff. In retaliation, the works would find fault with the next locomotive received for overhaul from the complainant depot, by reporting the boiler as badly scaled up. Proverbially, the pot was ever apt to call the kettle black.

To act as the intermediary between the two departments, Maunsell appointed a determined character, Tommy Brand, to have charge of all locomotive repairs. No locomotive was sent to works without his approval. In BR days, each Region had a Shopping Bureau with elaborate records, wall charts and what-have-you. Tommy, in his time, with his little black notebook, was a walking shopping bureau. He had been a locomotive fitter and a depot foreman on the LBSC, and knew all the tricks of the trade. For a fitter to be torn off a strip by Mr Brand for causing a locomotive failure was a worse punish-ment than any paper reprimand.

An edict went forth, in Maunsell's reign, that a locomotive de-railed, wholly or partially, must be sent to works before return to service for a precautionary check of weight distribution and spring adjustment by means of a weighbridge. To save time, the depots were allowed to arrange this direct either with Eastleigh or Ashford Works. The door was thereby opened to some quiet collusion between depots and works, so when a newly-repaired loco did give trouble, it could be sent back to works 'for weighing' without undue publicity: the fact that the works kept the loco for several days, rather longer than for a simple weighing operation, was neither here nor there!

Eastleigh, like other large railway workshops, supplied a whole host of items for every department: signal and track components, office furniture, station barrows, tablet pouches, horse harness; in the words of an eminent Works Manager, an order for a million mousetraps would be welcomed. The first automatic carriage washing installations were designed and made there, and the gas-works continued to provide gas for restaurant car kitchens long after carriage lighting changed over to electricity, the gas being distributed to outstations by special gas wagons.

When the last Schools class had been built, there were predictions that, with the rapid progress of electrification on the Southern, Eastleigh would get no more orders for new steam locomotives. Indeed, had it not been for Hitler's war, electric trains might have been running to Southampton and Bournemouth in the 1940s. In 1935, it began to look as if some relics of the steam era would be worthy of preservation, and the idea was approved by Maunsell. The oldest locomotive on the Southern, the ex-Isle of Wight Rly 2-4-0T *Ryde* built in 1864, had been standing idle at Eastleigh Works as nobody had the heart to scrap such a veteran, along with Dugald Drummond's single-wheeler Inspection Saloon, and together they were placed in the disused paint shop to form the nucleus of the Eastleigh Museum. Other relics were discovered in odd corners: an original Giffard injector, a Beattie flywheel steam feed pump, a pair of early wooden-centred coach wheels and a variety of nameplates and locomotive builders' plates. It was proposed to add the old Bodmin & Wadebridge coach which for many years stood in the centre of the concourse at Waterloo. However, in 1940 the urgent call for scrap metal for war purposes resulted in the disappearance of all but a few small items, including the elaborate LBSCR Royal Train decorations, and these were eventually taken over by the BR Curator of Historical Relics.

After the Grouping, Eastleigh became the sole supplier of all iron and brass castings. The latest pattern of continuous casting plant of French manufacture was installed in due course, largely to cope with the thousands of brake blocks consumed by the frequent stopping of the electric suburban trains, and a metallurgical laboratory was set up, to replace the rule-of-thumb methods which had prevailed in the making of castings. An amusing illustration of the latter arose when Maunsell ordered a thorough investigation into the wear of cylinders and piston rings. It came to light that the cylinders of the

Arthurs Nos 448–457 built at Eastleigh wore less than those of any others, and analysis of the cast iron proved it to have an unusual phosphorus content, making the iron hard and wear-resistant. The foundry foreman was asked to explain, and after searching through a dog-eared notebook he was able to discover that a large batch of scrap permanent-way chairs had been melted down at the time the cylinders had been cast. A chair of similar age was then examined in the laboratory and found to have an identical phosphorus content!

In 1846 the Directors of the South Eastern Railway decided to purchase 185 acres of land at Ashford, Kent, on which to lay the foundations of a 'Locomotive Establishment'. By 1850, there had been constructed two separate workshops for locomotives and for carriages and wagons, together with a complete housing estate. Known as Newtown, it was a model village of its kind, and comprised 132 railway houses each provided with the modern form of lighting by a railway gas-works. Ashford was limited in size to the building and repair of medium-size locomotives and continued to function until the end of steam. After grouping, the carriage work was transferred to Lancing and to Eastleigh.

Brighton Works, founded in 1852, had been built on the side of a hill, with the main station on one side and with a goods yard below. Over the years extensions had been added at different levels, inconvenient for moving material from one section to another, and there was no road access to the erecting and machine shops. When, in its last years in the 1960s, space was rented to a firm assembling light cars, these had to leave the works on rail wagons. Maunsell decided to dispense with the use of Brighton and the locomotive repair work was divided between Eastleigh and Ashford. The works stood almost empty from 1934 until 1940 when it was re-opened to provide for additional war work and to maintain repair facilities in the event of bomb damage at the other workshops.

Lancing had been built in 1912 to deal with carriages and wagons, to relieve the congestion at Brighton. In Southern days it was the centre of all the carriage overhauls, leaving Eastleigh Carriage Works to concentrate upon new construction. A complete overhaul was achieved in 25 working days, and 2,500 coaches were dealt with annually. Lancing was closed in 1965.

The transfer of the repair of the ex-LBSC locomotives to Eastleigh and Ashford in 1932 had an odd sequel. On commencing work on the first arrivals, the receiving works asked to be provided with the necessary drawings, in order that the dimensions of the working parts could be repaired in conformity with designed dimensions.

The reputation of Brighton suffered a severe blow when it was discovered not only that many drawings were missing but, worse, few of the engines bore much resemblance, other than outwardly, to such drawings as did exist!

Besides its comparative cheapness to build, the steam locomotive was economical in spares; all cast-iron, bronze, brass and white-metal could be recovered and re-used. Practically all the spare parts could be made at Eastleigh and Ashford, at short notice if necessary: there were few problems of purchasing parts from outside manufacturers. Spare parts were transported to and from the depots by carrying them on the backs of tenders. The method was well organised, to ensure that the injector from Ashford for an N class at Exeter and the brake valve from Eastleigh for a Schools at Ramsgate were changed over from engine to engine en route to their destination. Oil was recovered by a special washing plant at Eastleigh Works to which all dirty cloths were sent. Every engineman was supplied daily with one new and one washed cloth, to be returned after duty. The washed cloths were then used by the engine cleaners, and eventually found their way back, with the dirty new ones, to Eastleigh. The recovered oil was found suitable for wagon bearings and suchlike.

The growing Electrical Department called for specialised workshops to deal with electric motors and control equipment, and these existed at Durnsford Road, Selhurst and Peckham Rye, and Slade Green in addition to the facilities at the main carriage workshops. A smaller specialised workshop at Stewarts Lane dealt with the lighting equipment on steam-hauled coaching stock.

The Locomotive Running Department

The locomotive depots as they existed in 1937 are listed herewith, and the number of locomotives allocated to each one, in July of that year. The home depots of Arthurs (N15), Schools (V) and Nelsons (LN) are also shown.

London Area

Bricklayers Arms (121) N15, V.
Situated in the well-known goods yard, in the old SER buildings. New repair shop added 1934. Inconvenient location for light engines to and from Charing Cross, Cannon Street and London Bridge. 36-ton breakdown crane.
Sub-shed: *Ewer Street (Southwark)* for turning, coaling and watering.

Stewarts Lane (141) N15, LN.
Longhedge. Old SER and LCDR buildings; convenient for Victoria. Absorbed (1934) former LBSCR *Battersea Park* roundhouse depot. 20-ton breakdown crane.

Nine Elms (123) N15, LN.
Spacious ex-LSWR buildings in large goods yard, serving Waterloo. 36-ton breakdown crane.

Hither Green (45).
Modern SR building (1933) near marshalling yard. Absorbed some freight locomotives ex-*Bricklayers Arms*.

New Cross Gate (64).
Old LBSC buildings, unsuitable for largest locomotives.

Norwood (48).
Modern SR building (1935) near marshalling yard. Absorbed *West Croydon* and some freight locomotives ex-*New Cross Gate*.

Feltham (70).
Modern LSWR (1922) building in marshalling yard, replaced *Strawberry Hill.* 20-ton breakdown crane.
Sub-shed: *Ascot* closed 1937.

Kent
Gillingham (52).
Old LCDR buildings.
Sub-depot: *Faversham* (31).

Ramsgate (41) N15, V.
Modern SR depot (1930) replaced *Margate, Ramsgate Harbour,* and *Deal* depots. 15-ton breakdown crane.

Dover Marine (50).
Modern SR depot (1928) alongside beach, replaced *Dover Priory* and *Harbour* depots.
Sub-shed: *Folkestone Junction* for harbour branch locomotives.

Ashford (55).
Modern SR building (1931) replaced depot in main works. 36-ton breakdown crane.
Sub-shed: *Canterbury West.* (*Maidstone East* and *Maidstone West* closed 1933.)

Tonbridge (53).
Old SER building, restricted site.

Tunbridge Wells West (21).
LBSCR building.

Sussex
St Leonards (32) V.
LBSCR building at West Marina.
Sub-sheds: *Hastings* for turning, coaling and watering; *Bexhill West* for Crowhurst branch.

Eastbourne (25).
Best ex-LBSCR depot, spacious layout. Declined after 1933 electrification.

Newhaven Town (17).
Small LBSCR depot for boat traffic and port shunting.

Brighton (82).
LBSCR buildings. Awkward site. 36-ton breakdown crane.

Bognor Regis (18).
LBSCR building. Home depot of Atlantics on mid-Sussex line.
Sub-depot: *Littlehampton* (9).

Horsham (33).
LBSCR semi-roundhouse.
Sub-depot: *Three Bridges* (23).

Surrey
Redhill (28).
SER depot at strategic junction.

Guildford (89).
LSWR buildings, including semi-roundhouse. Cramped site.
Sub-sheds: *Ash* and *Bordon* (Hants).

Berkshire
Reading (17).
SER building.

Hampshire
Basingstoke (20).
LSWR building.

Eastleigh (105) N15.
LSWR buildings and enginemen's dormitory (1902). 36-ton break-down crane.
Sub-depots: *Andover Junction, Southampton Docks* (17).
Sub-sheds: *Winchester* (*Chesil* was GWR), *Southampton Terminus, Lymington.*

Fratton (72).
Portsmouth. Roundhouse formerly joint LBSC and LSWR. 36-ton breakdown crane.

Sub-depot: *Gosport.*
Sub-shed: *Midhurst.* Coal stage at *Hayling Island.*

Bournemouth Central (48).
LSWR building, modern engine hoist. Cramped site near station.
20-ton breakdown crane.
Sub-sheds: *Hamworthy Junction, Swanage.* (*Branksome* was LMS.)

Isle of Wight (27).
Ryde: main repair works, modern running shed.
Newport: Old IOWCR buildings.

Dorset

Dorchester (14).
Early LSWR building with dormitory house.
Sub-shed: *Weymouth* LSWR building demolished 1939. (Large
locomotives used *Weymouth* GWR depot for turning.)

Wiltshire

Salisbury (59) N15.
LSWR building. 36-ton breakdown crane.

Somerset

Yeovil (19).
Early LSWR building with turntable at Yeovil Junction.
Sub-shed: *Templecombe Upper.*

Devon

Exmouth Junction (112) N15.
Modern (1924) buildings replaced former *Exeter* (*Queen Street*) depot.
Workshop. 20-ton breakdown crane.
Sub-sheds: *Seaton, Lyme Regis, Exmouth, Okehampton, Bude.*

Barnstaple (18).
Old LSWR building.
Sub-sheds: *Torrington, Ilfracombe.*
(*Barnstaple Pilton Yard* (5) Lynton & Barnstaple depot closed 1935.)

Plymouth Friary (21).
LSWR building.

Sub-shed: *Callington* (Cornwall).

Cornwall

Wadebridge (7).
LSWR building.
Sub-shed: *Launceston*.

In the 1930s the salary paid to the man in charge of a locomotive depot ranged from £180 to £350 per annum according to size and importance of the place. He was granted a percentage in addition for emergency calls, but was paid no overtime. He had to be available at all hours, day and night, except for one day in the month, when he could be absent provided a colleague at a neighbouring depot would cover any calls. He had to live within easy distance of the depot, and he had to leave word where he could be found if he went to a cinema or visited friends. One simple way of being summoned was by a special engine whistle-code: an arrangement which suited ardent fisherman Tom S., often to be found in a boat about a mile offshore!

The greater proportion of depot buildings were pre-1900 and conversion from gas to electric lighting was not complete. Electric lamps on leads were gradually replacing the open-flame tallow-pot oil lamps used for working underneath an engine, or inside the boiler; a type of lamp in use in Ancient Egypt, its smoky flame causing one's clothes to reek, and cigarette to taste, of soot and paraffin. There was no heating in the sheds. Most of them were designed with one closed end where engines were berthed for repairs. The open end was permanently open for movements in and out; if there were any doors left, they had been clobbered so often as to render them inoperative! A few sheds were through-sheds open at both ends, wherein the continuous draught at least carried away the smoke. As no depot building was large enough to accommodate all its allocated stud of engines under cover, the staff were accustomed anyway to work in the open in all weathers. Boilersmiths were more fortunate, as a locomotive firebox was a snug, if cramped, place to work in on a cold day, and a favourite hiding place for a quiet game of cards. Work in a smokebox, however, was the filthiest and most unpopular task of all, especially as the washing facilities were limited to buckets of hot water drawn from an engine. Such luxuries as wash-rooms and clothes-drying rooms awaited the passing of the Factories Act of 1937.

The cynic would say that the conditions were tolerated because the railwayman had a secure job in times of high unemployment. To some extent that was true, of some men, but the majority found running shed life congenial. Open day and night, seven days a week, direct supervision was minimal and lenient, provided everyone 'mucked in' at the busy times. There was a strong loyalty, not to 'the Company' whose image was ever that of Scrooge, but to the depot: the feeling that the guv'nor must not be let down. Men off duty would not demur at being called to cover a mate who had gone sick. Drivers would nurse an ailing locomotive back home rather than leave it at another depot. With the aid of hosepipes, brooms and buckets of whitewash, the oldest of sheds could be kept clean and tidy. As ever, it was the teenagers who would run wild; a bevy of engine-cleaners armed with 'sockers'—cleaning clothes soaked in oil —was potentially explosive. They were best put to work on engines in different parts of the shed so that one gang was kept out of range of another. Newly-appointed welfare officers unacquainted with the genus engine-cleaner were shocked to find cleaners' mess-rooms devoid of glass in the windows. In the 1880s locomotives were commonly fitted with the Ramsbottom safety-valve, operated by a lever in the cab. The author's grandfather recalled a lad who would grab another's cap, put it on the safety-valve and, with a touch on the lever, shoot it up into the rafters, from which place, if the cap lodged there, the victim had to retrieve it.

A cleaner tempted to show off by moving an engine faced instant dismissal: cases had ended in tragedy. It was in 1859 that an engine escaped from the LBSCR shed at Petworth and ran some miles along the line, collecting a pair of crossing gates before being stopped. A cleaner was suspected of tampering with it. Thereafter, running sheds were provided with trap points to catch runaway engines.

No depot was complete without its allocation of cats: office cats, stores cats and half-wild ones with kittens in coal stacks. Harold Attwell, one of Maunsell's testing staff, recalled that a cat walked out of the coal when an Arthur was passing Woking on a Waterloo–Salisbury express. Pussy, presumably a Nine Elms resident, was consequently 're-allocated' to Salisbury shed.

Conditions at motive power depots deteriorated after World War II. With shortage of labour, pits and pathways were too often piled high with uncollected ashes; buildings went in need of attention, in some cases deferred pending a reconstruction scheme. Nine Elms was to be replaced by a new steam-cum-diesel depot at Clapham Junction; Bournemouth was to move to enlarged premises inside the Branksome Triangle; Tonbridge was to be rebuilt at the West

Yard, and so on. Understandably, expenditure was withheld owing to the uncertain future of steam but an atmosphere of neglect took hold.

Now, with a few exceptions, little remains of those former hives of activity; steam locomotive fitters and boilersmiths are a diminishing race. The good fitter was a versatile mechanic but the smith specialised in loco-type boilers, now scarce. One of his impressive arts was to take a light hammer and tap, one by one, a thousand stay-heads inside a firebox to tell which stays were sound and which were broken in the waterway.

The Nelson firebox was in shape virtually the same as the Ashford N class but enlarged, yet whereas stay breakage with the latter was no problem, the Nelsons suffered severely from it. Evidently, there was some unevenness in the expansion and contraction stresses which overloaded the stays in certain areas of the firebox.

The trouble was minimized by a change from copper to monel-metal stays and by using flexible stays in the throat-plate area.

A summary of the periodical and mileage examinations applicable to the Arthurs, Schools and Nelsons is given at the end of the chapter. The frequency and extent of such examinations or 'preventative maintenance' was a matter upon which locomotive engineers seldom agreed. During Maunsell's regime the temptation to add to the list because of one or two failures was resisted, and the philosophy of 'leaving well alone' prevailed, and was justified. The number of fitters to be employed at a depot was calculated according to the requirement of the types of engines allocated; one fitter was allowed for every six engines of Arthur and Schools class, and one for every five Nelsons. One boilersmith for ten engines was a rough average. For comparison it may be mentioned that it became necessary to have a fitter for every three of the original, unmodified Bulleid Pacifics, but even so, their availability was lower than the Nelsons.

The multi-cylinder Schools and Nelsons, unlike the Arthurs, could be allowed to run for 30 to 36,000 miles before the valves and pistons needed to be extracted, and, even then, the renewal of valve and piston rings was to ensure another period of reliable running rather than because they were near the limits of wear.

The boilers of the Schools were not at all troublesome, so that taken as a whole the maintenance of the Schools was the easiest of all. The larger pistons and heavier motion parts of the Arthur did not wear so well, and the thrust of the large outside cylinders gave the axle-boxes a good deal of punishment; consequently an Arthur would be likely to ride roughly after 20,000 miles or so. Unlike the Schools and

Nelsons, the axlebox guides were not fitted with adjusters (horn block wedges) to take up any knock, an omission which arose from the fear at the time the original Arthurs were designed that a maladjusted wedge could lock an axlebox in its guide and cause a derailment. That this fear was groundless was proved by experience with the Schools and Nelsons: the one alarming derailment of a Nelson's leading coupled wheels has been mentioned in Chapter 6.

In the maintenance of Arthurs, no depot could rival Bournemouth in the 1930s when the inimitable Joe Elliott had charge there. Joe, who had started life as a fitter, contended that Eastleigh Works did not fit axleboxes properly and whenever a newly-repaired Arthur arrived, he had it put under the hoist for the axleboxes to be made a tighter fit. The process would be repeated as and when a driver reported axlebox knock, so that Bournemouth Arthurs had a reputation for sweet running. To ensure that his Arthurs would run the 111 miles from Waterloo to Bournemouth West with an ample margin of water in the 5,000 gallon tenders, Joe would renew the piston rings frequently; in fact, he reckoned that his methods of maintenance rendered superfluous the compilation of mileage records. The day came when, in connection with some mishap in the London area, he was instructed to send to Waterloo the complete records of one of his engines, for the information of a Ministry of Transport Inspector. After some delay, the records were produced, all written in fresh ink. Suspicions being aroused, a few days later a high official arrived at Bournemouth without prior warning, demanding to see all the other records, after which it was Joe who went to Waterloo for a dressing-down.

A minor, but interesting alteration to the external appearance of the Arthurs, Schools and Nelsons was the removal, circa 1936–7, of the anti-vacuum valves on the smokeboxes. It was a fairly common practice everywhere to fit such valves, which were intended to admit air to the superheater and to the steam chest when coasting with regulator closed, to prevent the creation of a vacuum by the moving pistons which would draw ash, etc, from the smokebox into the cylinders. It had been noticed, particularly on the Arthurs, that slight carbonisation was occurring in the superheaters: this could only be the result of 'pumping back' from the steam chest: evidently, the anti-vacuum or snifting valves did not work. Practical tests proved thus to be so: the valves either remained firmly shut, or, at low speeds, 'chattered'.

Another theory behind the fitting of these valves was that the air admitted to the superheater would prevent excessive temperatures when no steam was passing to absorb the heat. In practice, with the regulator closed and the blastpipe not in operation, the amount of heat passing round the superheater elements was reduced. So the valves on Maunsell's engines were scrapped without any untoward consequences, and one wondered when other designers would come to the same conclusion; in due course, many did so.

Another fitting on the Arthurs, Schools and Nelsons to be abandoned was the crosshead-operated vacuum pump, intended to maintain vacuum when running without the use of the steam-operated ejector, and so save steam. The pumps would also maintain vacuum if the steam pressure was seriously reduced. The reasons for removing the pumps were that they were found to require frequent attention and air leakages could cause failures of the brake system.

SR Maintenance Examinations of Arthurs, Schools and Nelsons

Average monthly mileage 4–6,000 miles

Period or Mileage	Examine and Test: in steam, as necessary
10–14 days	Wash out boiler. Examine all accessible parts of boiler including waterways and tubes, ashpan, firebars and smokebox
Monthly	Boiler water gauges Driver's brake valve Vacuum limit valve and drip valves Cylinder drain cocks and gear Steam heating equipment (in season) Manifold stop cock
Two-monthly	Injectors, live and exhaust steam Clackboxes Vacuum brake system, and hand brake. Lubricators
Three-monthly	Test safety valves at full pressure Check pressure gauges against master gauge Renew firebox fusible plugs
Six-monthly	Measure and record tyre profiles and thickness Main frames and wheels Empty and clean out tenders

No 914 *Eastbourne*, of the second series in October 1932
(autographed by the designer).

"Keep the name bright"—No 914 on exhibition at Eastbourne
station./*Eastbourne Chronicle*

Top: No 909 *St Paul's* at Charing Cross, 1930./*LPC*

Above: No A895, later 1895, one of the three-cylinder U1 class
superceded by Schools on the Portsmouth line./*BR*

No 932 *Blundells* with high-sided tender, in smart condition as
maintained by Bournemouth depot, 1938./*C. R. L. Coles*

No 928 *Stowe* glides down West Stafford bank near Dorchester
with the Weymouth portion of the 12.30pm ex-Waterloo in 1938.
Engine and train are malachite green./*Author*

Sectional model of Schools, used for enginemen's instruction.

No 914 at Bournemouth, newly released from Eastleigh Works
with Lemaitre blastpipe and chimney, 1938./*Author*

"Whew"—Bournemouth fitters Alf Saunders and Cecil Knott
looking for trouble in the smokebox of No 914./*Author*

No 928 *Stowe* as now preserved at Beaulieu./*John Gillings*

No 930 *Radley*, in wartime black, steel plate in cab window and night-time anti-glare sheets in readiness, 1943. The Lemaitre chimney now has a rim./*SR*

No 934 *St Lawrence*, damaged during the London blitz, now (1948) has the first pattern of BR livery./*Author*

No 783 *Sir Gillemere* in 1941, fitted with three chimneys as an anti-aircraft measure. /*BR*

The coaling plant at Nine Elms in 1947 shows evidence of wartime bomb blasts. Seen is No 456 *Sir Galahad./R. E. Vincent*

No 30851 *Sir Walter Raleigh,* glistening in the snow, meets an uncleaned 'Packet' on a wintery morning near Pirbright, 1950./ *J. B. Heyman*

12,500 miles	Examine in position: Connecting rods and big-ends, Coupling rods, Crossheads, Crank axles, Valve gear, Reverser, Drawgear, Bogie, Buffers, Springs Withdraw underfeed journal oil pads, all axle-boxes
25,000 miles (Arthurs) 36,000 miles (Schools and Nelsons)	Examine after dismantling: Connecting rods and big-ends, Coupling rods, Crank axles and crank pins, Crossheads Withdraw valves and pistons. Renew rings. Decarbonise ports and steam passages. Check cylinder relief valves, drain cocks, etc Other parts for attention as reported by Drivers. Brake blocks to be replaced as required by adjustments. Drivers to renew worsted trimmings and siphon corks
Annually	Boiler examination by H.O. Boiler Inspector. Tubes to be withdrawn as directed by B.I., for examination for corrosion

In the wisdom of Sir Herbert Walker the management of the Locomotive Running Department and its staff of some 8,000 was vested in a chief officer who was independent, and not subservient either to operating or technical interests, which were liable to conflict. Internal policy, staff negotiations and disciplinary measures were in the hands of officers who had been trained at a locomotive works and had practical experience in charge of depots; however exalted, they were quite capable of putting on old clothes and taking a trip on the footplate. Bowler hats were a mark of rank and a protection against coal falling off tenders. It was an era noticeably free from militant action, for which some credit was due to an influential body of senior drivers who believed in settling grievances by constitutional methods, and to the Locomotive Inspectors, all ex-drivers, who were the diplomatic intermediaries between authority and the enginemen.

The senior inspector, John Watson, was an outstanding character. In his younger days as a driver at Nine Elms he had been invited to stand for election to the executive committee of his trade union and to declare certain lines of policy in his election manifesto. That did not suit John, who circulated a portrait of himself with the words 'J. Watson—Your Candidate'. He was elected at face value.

An advantage of the relatively small area of the Southern system was that Waterloo was within a day's journey from all parts. Officers and inspectors frequently met to discuss common problems, on an informal basis, with the station's 'Long Bar' as the meeting place. Locomotive men were reputedly a thirsty lot, but a sharp eye was kept for any abuses, and for any drivers booking on duty in an unfit state. All engines had a tray near the firehole door on which a bottle of tea or cocoa was kept warm. Smoking on the footplate was against regulations. In practice, a little latitude was allowed provided no liberties were taken, and provided an engine was not left un-attended when a driver slipped out for refreshment. It was hot work in high summer, and at one time on the LSWR enginemen were supplied during a heat-wave with a cooling drink of water mixed with oatmeal, by arrangement with the refreshment rooms at the principal stations.

The most serious disciplinery cases were, of course, those of passing signals at danger. Decisions about a driver's future career, whether in the interests of safety he should be confined to shunting work, always involved a great deal of heart-searching, especially concerning an experienced man having an otherwise clean record. There could be no hesitation in fitting locomotives with smoke deflectors, clumsy as they might appear, if thereby one cause of signal errors could be eliminated.

A driver might call himself lucky if he reached retiring age with-out committing some minor offence such as forgetting to stop at a station; however, only a small percentage was involved in a longer list of errors which could eventually, by the totting-up process, result in a reduction to shed work. A considerable proportion could boast that they had never been late for duty. Some had to admit that, thanks to an accommodating signalman, their sins had not reached the ears of authority. A Brighton-bound driver in the middle of the night found himself diverted to the Eastbourne line at Keymer Junction; he was at fault for taking signals for, and the signalman for setting up, the wrong route. After stopping, he sent his fireman back to the signalbox, where the signalman was found asleep. After breaking a few more rules about wrong-line working and reporting of irregularities, the train went on its proper course and the delay was suitably covered up.

If the telephone system was rather ineffective, the grape-vine

certainly was not, and naturally some tit-bits got relayed to management level, and the officers were wise to keep their ears open.
Evidence obtained through the grape-vine could hardly be used for
disciplinary action, but it did sometimes reveal the truth.

Occasionally irregularities were reported by the public and one
example had a sad ending. There were complaints of poaching on the
Meon Valley line. Examination of signalbox records threw suspicion
on a pick-up freight train and the length of time it had taken between
two stations on certain days. An inspector then found a train stopped
and unattended in mid-section, and on blowing the engine-whistle
the driver, fireman and guard came out of the woods, with rabbit-
nets. The case was still *sub judice* when the driver took his own life.
Rabbits on railway embankments were considered fair game when
shot from the footplate.

Shortage of water in the boiler, with fusing of the lead plugs, was
another serious crime, in view of the risks involved. The fireman
may have been at fault, but on principle it was the driver who had to
take the rap. There were quite a few cases of damaged fireboxes
each year from this cause, but in only one instance, involving a
Nelson, did the crown of the firebox collapse and the fireman was
blown onto the tender and killed.

Inspecting Officers of the then Ministry of Transport had the
right to investigate all mishaps involving injury or risk of injury to
the public and cases of injury to the staff, whether serious or slight.
Their activities, although limited to making recommendations for
preventive action, had a wholly beneficent influence and were
always conducted with fairness and impartiality. They held footplate permits and could, by arrangement, ride on any engine they
wished.

A steady flow of applications from members of the public for footplate trips was received at Locomotive Running Headquarters. Some
of them were difficult to refuse: for example, the person who wrote
'I am about to retire after holding a first-class season ticket on your
railway for 25 years, and I would like to make my last journey on the
engine!' Requests usually had to be declined, as the official view,
supported by the Ministry, was that the presence of a stranger
might, by his getting in the way or speaking at the wrong moment,
interfere with the vigilance of the engine crew. Drivers were for-
bidden to let anybody, railwaymen included, ride on the engine
without a permit. It was not unknown, of course, for the rule to be
broken by some kind-hearted driver. One such was persuaded by a
keen amateur to let him ride from Charing Cross to Ashford but

while he was on the engine the suitcase he had left in the train was stolen, so the cat was out of the bag and the driver got three days' suspension from duty.

It was only necessary for a driver to receive a verbal caution from somebody in authority, for a warning to circulate rapidly through the jungle telegraph. For example, a certain superintendent rode in a train from Waterloo to Reading, and on alighting he commented to the driver that he heard no whistle warnings given as required at public crossings. So far as he was concerned, that was the end of the matter, but within 48 hours a formal request was submitted through the staff committee at a depot many miles away, asking for the line-side whistle boards in that area to be repainted. Posting admonitory notices in the depot notice-cases never had the same effect.

The summer months up to 1939 were hectic ones for the loco-motive department. Extra trains to cope with holiday traffic began in May, and the summer timetable was introduced a month earlier than the other group companies. Leave for the enginemen was spread out between April and October to minimise the number of men absent at one time. Additional cleaners, to permit the upgrad-ing of permanent cleaners to firemen, and firemen to drivers, were taken on for the period and stood off during the winter. Engine repairs were brought forward or deferred in order to have the maximum number available. Gone are the Saturday queues at Waterloo which filled the station concourse and started outside in the road below; no longer are empty trains kept in readiness in every available siding within a 30-mile radius of London, nor spare loco-motives at vantage points such as Tonbridge, Redhill, Horsham, Guildford and Basingstoke where assistance might be required.

All the principal trains would be run in two or more portions. The 11am Waterloo–West of England, for example, had four relief trains departing before and after the advertised time, and the choice of locomotive for each train required careful judgement. On hand there would be the weekday 11am engine, a Nelson, a Scotch Arthur, a Salisbury Arthur, a 'Paddleboat' and a Feltham S15 temporarily uprated from freight work. These would have to be shuffled so that the early departures would be certain to show the others a clean pair of heels. The driver who had been given the 'Paddleboat' would spot E. S. Moore, the Divisional Locomotive Superintendent, standing on the end of No 11 platform, climb off the engine, and expostulate about the load of the train, the weather, the inexperience of the fireman, the doubtful quality of the coal and the condition of the engine. E.S.M. would listen patiently, remove his pince-nez glasses, studiously clean them and, when the flow of words ceased, grunt: "I expect you'll do your best". The driver, having relieved the pressure of his feelings like the release of steam from the safety valves, would grin and get his train away in good style.

There were 'Black Saturdays' when some little incident would cause delays to escalate. A driver would discover, just before starting time, that the regulation minimum of 19½in of vacuum could not be held with the small ejector, and a posse of carriage examiners and station staff would frantically search for the cause of the leakage. An Arthur once started off and then, with the train barely out of the platform, a coupling parted, whereupon a coil of wire binding, unravelling from the torn vacuum hose-pipes, short-circuited the live rail. No wonder E.S.M. kept hanging on the wall of his office the poker-work motto: 'No sooner have you made ends meet, than somebody moves the ends'.

The most complicated exercises in locomotive diagramming were those connected with annual events such as Ascot and Epsom Races and the Aldershot Tattoos, to which, in steam days, trains converged from all points of the compass. After arrival, and within a limited time before the homeward journeys, every locomotive had to run light to one or other of the nearer locomotive depots for servicing. They then had to be returned to their trains, which were marshalled in correct sequence of departure on one of the running lines. They were field days for the supervision staff and for the breakdown crews who were held in readiness at key points. Long practice in coping with those events was to prove invaluable when the Southern was called upon, in 1940, to cope with over 385,000 troops, of several nationalities, landed at South Coast ports following the fall of Dunkirk and the collapse of France. Coaching stock of all four Group Companies was mustered to form 200 trains by which the men were dispersed all over the United Kingdom. On that occasion, many drivers, firemen and guards were on duty continuously for 24 hours at a stretch. At one of the locomotive depots at a key point, Redhill, so many engines were being serviced that the yard became for a time completely blocked with mountains of ashes. For all the veteran Southern locomotives which were pressed into service, it was their finest hour!

The Arthurs,
Schools and Nelsons at Work

At every depot there were a few speed-merchants amongst the drivers, ready to attempt an unofficial record when egged on by a provocative argument in the mess-room or by some private enthusiast who made it known that he was travelling in the train with stop-watches. They would have liked the opportunity of trying out Southern engines on the main-lines to the North where there was greater scope for uninterrupted high-speed running than on their home ground, an opportunity which one or two drivers were able to enjoy to the full during the locomotive exchanges of 1948, though not with any of Maunsell's engines. Occasionally, train-running logs published in the *Railway Magazine* revealed that liberties had been taken with the schedules and, if minutely analysed, with speed restrictions. To these displays, higher authority turned a blind eye whenever they chanced to read the popular railway press. The *Railway Gazette* catered for professional railwaymen and did not publish information which did not bear the stamp of officialdom.

Although it had occurred a quarter of a century before, the disaster at Salisbury in 1906 when an up Plymouth boat special was wrecked by excessive speed still lingered in the memories of former LSWR staff, and a Board Minute which required all trains to stop at Salisbury was still in force. All down trains were likewise restricted at Poole, because of the sharp curve preceded by a steep down gradient. Members of the Chief Civil Engineer's Office travelled the system to detect track irregularities, and to check up on the observance of speed limits. Their presence in a reserved compartment was often spotted by the guard in time to give the driver the tip, but firm action was taken against drivers who were caught. Special watch was kept on sharp curves following complaints by gangers that the track was being pushed out of alignment by somebody unable to tell the difference between 15mph and 35mph.

The curve at the west end of Tonbridge station was a good deal sharper than it is now, and as non-stop trains approached at high speed in both directions with a long bank to follow in the up direction, drivers were always tempted to rush it. The Arthur and Nelson 4-6-0s had thinner flanges on the centre pair of coupled wheels to ease the negotiation of curves; nevertheless at other than slow speeds, those engines were apt to go round with a series of jerks as if the curve consisted of a series of short straights. With the introduction of flange-oilers or greasers, fitted to the rail, the effect was greatly reduced as well as the wear of rails and flanges.

In 1927 the 11am Waterloo–West of England was given the title of the 'Atlantic Coast Express', which was abbreviated to the 'ACE'. The Arthurs proved capable of keeping the 86min schedule to Salisbury, 83·8 miles, with ease. This irked some eager drivers at Nine Elms, one of whom, Fred Stickley with his favourite Arthur No 777 *Sir Lamiel* (colloquially known as the Austin 7 or Pile of 7s), ran to Salisbury in under 75 minutes. Officialdom was *not* amused. The story went that Stickley was summoned to headquarters and severely reprimanded by the Locomotive Running Superintendent. On leaving that dignitary's office, somewhat crestfallen, he was then escorted along the corridor to the Chief Mechanical Engineer's office and warmly congratulated for proving what a Maunsell Arthur could do. But the 86min schedule remained.

The same locomotive, No 777, was involved in a fine run in the up direction with the 'ACE', as reported in the *Railway Magazine* for June 1936. The 90min allowance from Salisbury to Waterloo was cut by 17¼ minutes. Over the 65½ miles from Grateley to Wimbledon, the average was 79.6mph; over the 33½ miles from Worting Junction to Esher, 82.7mph. Maxima were 88½mph at Andover and 90mph at Byfleet.

During the 1930s accelerated schedules were introduced on the other Group Companies, culminating in the high speed running of the 'Silver Jubilee' on the LNER. The Southern kept to a policy of regular-interval expresses at speeds well within the capability of the locomotives. Waterloo applauded when *Punch* published a cartoon in which a passenger, alighting from his train unexpectedly before time, was seen making a bee-line for the buffet in order to put the time saved to good purpose.

Drivers were not entirely deprived of opportunities for speed, as the Southern schedules did not have built-in recovery times, and drivers were instructed to regain time.

The Urie Arthurs, as might be expected, never did anything very spectacular. In 1930, Nos 736–755 were distributed thus: Nine Elms 9, Eastleigh 2, Bournemouth 2, Salisbury 2, and Exmouth Junction 5. They were generally used on the semi-fast services, and on Southampton boat trains, van trains and specials. They worked passenger trains on the Portsmouth direct line until electrification, after which Nine Elms transferred five to Eastleigh.

The Eastleigh Arthurs, Nos 448–457, had a settled existence at Salisbury. It was Southern practice to keep particular engines to the same depot as far as practicable, and thus to encourage a depot to look after its own, for anybody's engine was likely to become nobody's care. These Arthurs worked the main-line in both directions and with particular success over the switchback Salisbury–Exeter line, over which the non-stop trains like the 'ACE' were allowed 96 minutes for the 88 miles. Two minutes more were allowed in the up direction. The load for the schedule was 11 bogies, and the Salisbury Arthurs could take 14 bogies when pressed.

The following examples of good runs may be quoted from Cecil J. Allen's articles on British Locomotive Practice and Performance which appeared in the *Railway Magazine*:

No 452 with 10 coaches, 345 tons full, non-stop

Salisbury–Templecombe	28.5 miles	32min 20sec
Templecombe–Yeovil Jct	10.8 miles	9min 25sec
Yeovil Jct–Axminster	22.0 miles	19min 55sec
Axminster–Sidmouth Jct	14.7 miles	18min 50sec
Sidmouth Jct–Exeter Central	12.0 miles	11min 35sec

The net time was 92min and a top speed of 80mph was exceeded at Gillingham, Sherborne, Axminster and Broadclyst.

No 453 with 13 coaches, 450 tons full, non-stop

Salisbury–Templecombe	28.5 miles	31min 53sec
Templecombe–Yeovil Jct	10.8 miles	9min 19sec
Yeovil Jct–Axminster	22.0 miles	20min 32sec
Axminster–Sidmouth Jct	14.7 miles	19min 23sec
Sidmouth Jct–Exeter Central	12.0 miles	18min 40sec

Note: *Signal checks at Axminster and approaching Exeter.*

No 451 with 11 coaches, 375 tons full, non-stop

Exeter Central–Sidmouth Jct	12.0 miles	16mins	12 sec
Sidmouth Jct–Axminster	14.7 miles	14min	20sec
Axminster–Yeovil Jct	22.0 miles	23min	6sec
Yeovil Jct–Templecombe	10.8 miles	11min	20sec
Templecombe–Salisbury	28.5 miles	29min	57sec

For comparison, in 1926, Urie Arthur No 747 worked the up 'ACE' with 350 tons full, thus:

Exeter Central–Sidmouth Jct	12.0 miles	15min	50 sec
Sidmouth Jct–Axminster	14.7 miles	15min	40sec
Axminster–Yeovil Jct	22.0 miles	21min	55sec
Yeovil Jct–Templecombe	10.8 miles	12min	20sec
Templecombe–Salisbury	28.5 miles	31min	25sec

The train was stopped by signals at Templecombe. Allowing for that, the net time was 93min. It was on this journey that Mr Allen clocked 90mph for the first time on the Southern.

In 1934, Scotch Arthur No 768 made a brilliant run with 460 tons full, in the down direction, in spite of rain and headwinds, thus:

Salisbury–Templecombe	28.5 miles	32min	55sec
Templecombe–Yeovil Jct	10.8 miles	9min	15sec
Yeovil Jct–Axminster	22.0 miles	19min	50sec
Axminster–Sidmouth Jct	14.7 miles	16min	35sec
Sidmouth Jct–Exeter Central	12.0 miles	11min	25sec

The overall time was 90min, with 82mph at Gillingham, 85 at Sherborne, 80 at Chard Junction, 86.5 at Axminster and 83 at Broadclyst.

It was the practice in Southern days to change engines at Salisbury in both directions. The pros and cons of doing so were often debated; whilst ostensibly through-working would have improved the daily mileage run by some engines, instances were limited whereby the round trip could be made in the day and so balance the out-and-home engine workings. The same difficulty was encountered, in securing long-mileage daily duties for the main-line diesel-electric locomotives in the 1950s. Lodging turns, and hence through-working of engine crews, had been abolished, so Salisbury had become a changeover point for enginemen. The change of engines as well, was in keeping with the principle of keeping engines and crews together on the top-link duties. If thereby the maximum possible mileage was not obtained out of the engines their appearance and condition gained, and the enginemen got more satisfaction out of their work.

The early allocation of the 'Scotsmen', Nos 763–792, was, roughly speaking, the first ten to Stewarts Lane, the second ten to Nine Elms and the last ten to Bournemouth. After 1933, approximately half of them were on the Eastern section and half on the Western. The small-tender Arthurs No 793–806 from 1926 to 1933 worked on the Central section, where they were matched against the LBSCR Baltics (afterwards rebuilt to N15/x class) and proved the better engines. The N15/x class turned out to be no better than the Urie N15. After the Central section electrification Nos 793–806 went to the Eastern section where they remained until their end. From 1926 until 1937 Nos 783–792 formed a team which operated most successfully from Bournemouth. The later numbers displaced by Schools then went to Exmouth Junction.

The first depots to have Schools were Dover and Deal in May and June of 1930. In September Deal was closed with the opening of the new Ramsgate depot. It had a band of main-line drivers who had been working the accelerated Folkestone–Charing Cross trains in great style with the L1 4-4-0s and they proceeded to show what could be done with Schools. In the same year Eastbourne, another depot with a reputation for able drivers and well-kept engines, introduced Schools to the fast trains to and from Victoria. In 1931, Ramsgate had Nos 900–903, 905 and 906, Eastbourne Nos 904, 907–909 but in July the latter were sent to St Leonards to start the Schools on the Tonbridge–Hastings route. Their success already obvious, an order for twenty more was agreed upon. By the end of 1933, all the first ten had been sent to St Leonards, and Nos 910–923 were at Ramsgate.

When the first batch of Schools was being built, scrapping was taking place of some of the lower-powered 4-4-0s. All 43 of the Brighton B2x class were to be cut up, ten of the Ashford B1 class, and the Ashford F1 class was steadily diminishing. Likewise on the Western section the Drummond C10 class of ten engines was eliminated, together with 49 of Adams' express 4-4-0s. Whilst many of them had become surplus to requirements, others had reached the limit of economic repair, and their place had been filled by remaining 4-4-0s. Before the second batch of twenty Schools was finished, a case had been made for increasing the batch to thirty, making forty Schools in all. Nos 924–933 were earmarked for the Western section, and Nos 934–939 were given to Bricklayers Arms to supplement the others already working on the Eastern section.

Nos 924–933 were allocated to Fratton depot for working the Portsmouth–Waterloo trains. They were suited to the size of the roundhouse at Fratton, and at the end of the up journey to Waterloo they could be turned there, on a turntable formerly on the north side, and serviced in the sidings on the south side of the station which went by the familiar name of The Beach, thus avoiding the light run to Nine Elms depot. The Beach is now a berth for electric stock.

Prior to the arrival of the Schools, Maunsell's U1 class three-cylinder 2-6-0s had been tried on the Portsmouth line with rather poor results—surprisingly, because on paper they were slightly more powerful than the Schools and with six wheels of 6ft 0in diameter they should have had an advantage on the 1 in 80 gradients. On the other hand, their boilers were inferior in pressure, grate area and heating surface, and could barely sustain the non-stop run down to Woking, let alone the harder work south of Guildford. On the Maunsell Moguls the leading bissel truck was connected to the frame with a Cartazzi slide, a device with two opposite-sloping wedges on each mating face which provided a self-centring action. It also allowed the Moguls to sway rather freely at the front end, which on the U1 was in the form of a box above the buffer beam known as the piano. When running downhill from Buriton Tunnel to Havant on reverse curves, the view from the footplate of the piano rocking from side to side was a little disconcerting.

The Schools rode sweetly through curves and climbed the gradients even better than the Arthurs. On non-stop trains between Waterloo and Portsmouth in both directions, a Schools was allowed 90 minutes with a maximum of 11 coaches. Non-stop electric trains are today allowed four minutes more.

In 1937 electrification of the Portsmouth line via Guildford displaced the Schools from Fratton. The freight and van trains continued to be worked by steam, as elsewhere, and the number of locomotives rendered redundant was not such as to warrant any scrapping, surplus locomotives being put into store. This was just as well, as the events of 1939 onwards were to prove.

Nos 924–933 were then sent to Bournemouth. The trains on the Bournemouth services were heavy, especially in the summer, and included some non-stop expresses over the 108 miles. Only three speed restrictions below 60mph existed: 40mph at Worting Junction on the down line; 15mph at Northam curve, Southampton; and 40mph over the old bridge and causeway crossing the river Test at Redbridge. The Arthurs at Bournemouth had been great favourites with their drivers, and the tenders carried 5,000 gallons against the 4,000 gallons of a Schools. Even with a load limit of 10 coaches, the water supply was only marginally sufficient for non-stop working. Once again, Arthurs and Schools were to be matched, this time under more difficult conditions; moreover the traffic department had a habit of adding a couple of extra coaches at short notice. The Bournemouth men took up the challenge, and in the *Railway Magazine* for September 1939, Cecil J. Allen was able to say 'the phenomenon of Southern locomotive performance is the place that has been taken by the Schools which display tractive powers by no means inferior to the King Arthur 4-6-0s, and not far short of those of the larger Lord Nelson engines'. He went on to quote specimen runs such as:

No 926 Repton, 14 coaches equal to 490 tons full; one stop, at Southampton

Waterloo–Surbiton	12 miles	18min	9sec
Surbiton–Woking	12.4 miles	13min	7sec
Woking–Basingstoke	23.4 miles	28min	3sec
Basingstoke–Winchester	18.8 miles	18min	58sec
Winchester–Southampton	12.6 miles	14min	59sec*
Southampton–Bournemouth	28.8 miles	35min	44sec

* *Dead stop by signals at St Denys*

No 927 Clifton with 15 coaches equal to 525 tons full

Waterloo–Surbiton	17min 53 sec
Surbiton–Woking	12min 23sec
Woking–Basingstoke	25min 18sec
Basingstoke–Winchester	18min 2sec
Winchester–Southampton	14min 24sec

The present-day timing of 70min from Waterloo to Southampton with 12-coach electric trains seems less remarkable than 88min with

15 coaches when it is remembered that the 3,200 rated horsepower of the REP electric multiple-unit is nearly three times that of a Schools! And the electric train runs on roller bearings instead of the plain bearings of pre-war steam stock, and has electro-pneumatic brakes instead of vacuum brakes.

One slight concession made to the Schools was the limit of seven coaches up the 1 in 50 Upwey bank between Weymouth and Dorchester; Arthurs were allowed to take eight coaches, and Nelsons ten coaches, without a banking engine. Otherwise, apart from the 1 in 60 between Poole and Parkstone, the gradients were not difficult.

The zenith of the Schools was attained in 1938 when they were newly painted in light green livery, with coaching stock to match, for the 'Bournemouth Limited'. The train was as fine a sight as any of the famous trains in British railway history, and running non-stop in both directions between London and Bournemouth it was one of the longest runs regularly performed without taking water from track-troughs. Non-stop runs had commenced in 1899 and were never resumed after 1939. The 'Limited' ran to Weymouth, with a portion for Swanage and a Schools berthed overnight at Dorchester depot to start the up working from Weymouth next morning. So for one glorious year there flashed across the Wessex landscape a train which reflected the bright greens of the New Forest in summer, and which even on dull days held a glint of the 'Sunny South'.

With such talented rivals, the Lord Nelson class may not appear to have held the pride of place befitting the largest Southern express locomotives, but there was no doubt in the minds of the locomotive running foremen who, when confronted with a choice, would put a Nelson on the hardest and heaviest train. To illustrate the greater reserve of power in the Nelsons, the logs given of Schools with 500-ton trains can be compared with those of Nelsons made by Cecil J. Allen in the same period, 1937–1939, taken over the 35.8 mile stretch between Surbiton and Basingstoke. The 60mph limit in the London area ended at Surbiton and thence sustained power output was required. Three Nelson runs were with the 12-Pullman car 'Bournemouth Belle', 500 tons, and that of No 861 with a 14-coach 'Crusader' special, 515 tons.

No 864 *Sir Martin Frobisher* (Lemaitre-fitted)	34min 11sec
No 860 *Lord Hawke* (Kylchap-fitted)	35min 54sec
No 860 *Lord Hawke* (original)	36min 2sec

No 861 *Lord Anson* (original)	36min 40sec
No 927 *Clifton* (original)	37min 41sec
No 926 *Repton* (original)	41min 10sec

To round off the comparisons, twenty-four years later John Webber of Nursling clocked 31min 16sec with a rebuilt Merchant Navy on the 12-car Belle. Engine No 35005 *Canadian Pacific* was hot-footing it with Dr E. Rabbetts of Bournemouth on the eve of his retirement.

Let that keen observer of locomotive performance, O. S. Nock, make the final and impartial comment on the hey-day of Arthurs, Schools and Nelsons. 'The high morale of the Southern locomotive department,' he wrote,* 'was reflected not only in the fine tradition of enginemanship in the working of trains but in the smartness of turn-out of every passenger locomotive, at all depots from Ramsgate and Dover in the east to the smaller sheds in Devon and Cornwall, at a period when elsewhere in Britain standards of locomotive cleanliness were declining.'

Southern Steam, O. S. Nock. David & Charles, Newton Abbot. 1966.

CHAPTER TWELVE

The War and After

In the early summer of 1940 the Southern Railway found itself well and truly in the front line when the Nazis overran Belgium and France, and most of the territory became within a few minutes flying time of enemy airfields. Regular services were maintained everywhere, nevertheless, though on a reduced scale. Gone were the boat trains, excursion trains, Pullmans and most dining-cars. For a time, there were for once some Arthurs, Schools and Nelsons out of use. Cleaning and maintenance declined as the running sheds were pre-occupied with air raid precautions. Servicing engines in the blackout had to be carried on without lights, though hot ashes had to be dropped and firehole doors opened. Staff had to carry gas masks and steel helmets: during the invasion scare drivers asked to be provided with rifles on the footplate. Between July 1940 and August 1943 there were 58 daylight attacks on SR trains from the air, the majority in Kent. Only a few caused casualties; early on, Ramsgate driver Goldsack was killed by machine-gun bullets, and the CME promptly sought ways of protecting the enginemen.

A Schools class was taken in to Ashford Works and the cab was lined inside with a layer of asphalt as some protection against bullets, but it made the cab extremely cramped and gave no protection from attacks from behind, so the idea was dropped. The trail of steam from the chimney of a moving engine enabled the pilot of an aircraft to spot a potential target, so for the second experiment an Arthur was fitted with three chimneys and three blastpipes in order to see whether the escaping steam would thereby be more quickly dispersed, instead of forming one long trail. It was not particularly effective in doing so; what it did do, was to bring down quantities of soot from hitherto undisturbed areas of tunnel roofs, effectively blacking-out the front cab windows and much else. By that time, mid-1941, the menace had been reduced: enemy raiders did not have much chance of looking for moving targets, and preferred to drop their bombs on coastal towns and retreat quickly across the Channel. In one such attack on Deal, bombs fell on the station where a train was standing, killing Driver Cotton of Ramsgate, one of the expert Schools class drivers.

91

In all, 189 Southern locomotives were damaged by enemy action, but only one, 'Paddleboat' No 458, was too badly crippled to be worth repair. No 458 was hit by a bomb at Nine Elms depot during the London blitz of 1940–41, as also was a Nelson. No 855, and Schools No 934 was hit when standing on Cannon Street Bridge. Few running sheds escaped air-raid damage: the most seriously hit were Bricklayers Arms, Stewarts Lane, New Cross Gate, Nine Elms and Fratton. Five shedmasters received the British Empire Medal.

In 1942 ten Urie Arthurs were able to be spared to help the NE area of the LNER, Nos 739, 740/2/4/7/8/9, 750/1/4. They returned to the Southern in 1943 when military traffic was building up in preparation for Overlord, the Allied Invasion of Europe.

With the return of peacetime the Arthurs, Schools and Nelsons found themselves relegated to the 'second division'. The Bulleid Pacifics had by then appeared on the scene. Instead of the narrow fireboxes of the Maunsell engines, which demanded considerable technique in firing, the Pacifics had large, square fireboxes; they were easy to fire and would steam liberally, almost regardless of the skill of the fireman and the quality of the coal. By then, the National Coal Board controlled the distribution of fuel, and the railways could no longer buy from collieries of their choice. The customer was not offered a menu: he had to eat what he was given, and it was usually hash. The best loco coals went elsewhere, some to export markets.

In 1946 the Government sponsored a scheme to convert a proportion of the railways' locomotives to oil-firing. On the Southern it was decided to turn over to oil in the Eastleigh and Exmouth Junction districts, convenient for sea-borne supplies and in substitution for Welsh coals, in short supply, which those districts normally used. Thus it came about that a variety of locomotive classes operating in those districts had to be converted to oil, ranging from Urie Arthurs to T9s. Arthurs Nos 740/5/8/9 and 752 belonging to Eastleigh were converted, and performed very well with a weir-type burner fixed at the front of the firebox. Two West Country Pacifics so converted did not steam well with that arrangement, and trials with a burner in the centre of the grate were in hand when the Government ran into difficulties over oil supplies and the scheme collapsed. The first Arthur converted, No 740, worked the 11.30am Waterloo–Bournemouth on April 9th, 1947. Oil storage tanks, together with pumps and steam-heating equipment to make the crude oil fluid for delivery to the locomotive tender tanks, were installed at Eastleigh and Fratton, and preparatory work had been put in hand at Exmouth Junction, Barnstaple, Plymouth and Wade-

In 1949 No 30784 *Sir Nerovens* was fitted with an experimental spark-arrester, and became known as 'The Beefeater'. Seen at Battledown flyover on a down Bournemouth train./*R. E. Vincent*

No 30785 *Sir Mador de la Porte,* with Salisbury line headcode, thunders down through Clapham Jct past the tail-end of a BIL unit in 1949./*C. C. B. Herbert*

No 30768 *Sir Balin* working the short-lived all-Pullman 'Kentish Belle', near Reculvers in 1954./*P. Ransome-Wallis*

No 30789 *Sir Guy* drifts downhill past Upwey Wishing Well Halt towards Weymouth in 1950./*J. C. Flemons*

Ramsgate station and locomotive depot in steam days. No 30763
Sir Bors de Ganis backs an empty train into the Carriage Shed./
W. A. Corkill

Relegated to freight work, with a washout plug leaking water and
scale, No 30769 *Sir Balan* labours up Mildenborough bank, whilst
a Britannia Pacific skims downhill in 1953./*B. E. Morrison*

Last years of *Lord Nelson*—in BR livery No 30850 passes Worting Junction on a Bournemouth-York express./*D. Cross*

The last years of steam on the Hastings line. No 30924 *Haileybury* on a Charing Cross train at St Leonards (Warrior Square)./ *P. I. Rawlinson*

Along the Folkestone Warren, where the track had been stabilised against earth slips, runs No 30921 *Shrewsbury* with an up relief boat train in 1966; the headcode route is via Maidstone East./*D. Cross*

A Schools on a 'Royal' when HM The Queen visited the Medway Towns in 1956. No 30925 *Cheltenham* in appearance puts the clock back to pre-war days./*J. Head*

With closure of the Somerset and Dorset line imminent, (where the Schools class was never permitted to work), No 30932 *Blundells* heads a special into Bath, with a Class 2 4-4-0 carrying the tablet exchanger./*R. E. Toop*

Schools west of Salisbury—No 30925 *Cheltenham* leaves Sidmouth Junction with the 11.00am Exeter-Waterloo in September 1962./ *R. N. Joanes*

Top: No 917 *Ardingly* comes to grief at Catford in 1946./*Author*

Above: The trail of destruction at Catford seen from behind the
derailed locomotive./*Author*

No 851 *Sir Francis Drake* after ploughing along, engine and train derailed, at Byfleet, 1946./*SR*

Shawford, three-quarters of an hour after the derailment./*Author*

bridge. But all in vain: by the autumn of 1948 all the Urie Arthurs had been restored to coal-firing.

In the last year before nationalisation, 1947, the allocation of the Arthurs, Schools and Nelsons was approximately as follows:

King Arthurs

736–755 Nine Elms 4, Bournemouth 2, Eastleigh 9, Salisbury 3 and Exmouth Junction 2.

448–457 Salisbury.

763–792 Stewarts Lane 8, Nine Elms 9, Dover 5, Bournemouth 4 and Eastleigh 4.

793–806 Stewarts Lane 5, Ashford 6, Bricklayers Arms 2 and Hither Green 1.

Schools

All based on the Eastern Section at Stewarts Lane, Bricklayers Arms, Ramsgate, Dover and St Leonards. Locomotives Nos 928, 929 and 930 were based at Brighton for working to Salisbury on the Brighton–Cardiff and Brighton–Plymouth through trains.

Lord Nelsons

All based on the Western Section at Nine Elms 5, Eastleigh 8 and Bournemouth 3.

In 1953 the first Arthur to be scrapped was No 754; other Urie Arthurs were withdrawn year by year until 1958, when the last, No 738, disappeared. Their names, recast on new nameplates, were transferred to BR Class 5s but lost something of their significance in the process. To make up for the loss of Urie Arthurs from Eastleigh, all the Nelsons were concentrated in that district.

The Arthurs, Schools and Nelsons were obsolescent in 1948 and quite obsolete alongside the excellent BR Class 5s, easily serviced and maintained. Some enginemen even preferred a BR5 to a Merchant Navy on the 'Bournemouth Belle'. With 140 Pacifics there was, on paper, little justification for keeping so many Arthurs and Nelsons but the number of Pacifics available for service on any given day fluctuated wildly, and the Maunsell engines had to be held in reserve to make up deficiencies. The appearance of the first modified Pacific, Merchant Navy No 35018, in April 1956 marked the culmination of a long struggle with the shortcomings of the originals and, for the Regional officers involved, a long wait for approval from higher up. So the faithful Maunsell Arthurs, Schools and Nelsons were destined to linger on into the 1960s, outwardly somewhat decrepit but inwardly reliable to the end.

Up until 1946, the Arthurs, Schools and Nelsons had not been involved in any major mishaps. But in December of that year No 851 *Sir Francis Drake* and all twelve coaches of an up Weymouth train were completely derailed at speed approaching Byfleet station. The track beneath the train was torn up, but it came to rest upright and nobody was injured. The line was cleared quickly by the combined efforts of breakdown gangs from Nine Elms, Bricklayers Arms, Brighton and Guildford: it was the only occasion in Southern history when four steam cranes were seen together. Three months previously, No 917 *Ardingly* and the coaches of a Victoria–Ramsgate train had been derailed at Catford: the only fatality was an RAF pilot who had survived the Battle of Britain. Both accidents were the direct result of poor track conditions attributable to dirty ballast and poor drainage, brought about by the maintenance difficulties of the war years. In 1947, No 453 *King Arthur* on an up Salisbury train ran into the rear of an up Bournemouth train at Farnborough because of a signalman's error. *King Arthur* lay slain on his side but both driver and fireman got away with a bad shaking.

In July 1952, No 854 (by then, 30854) *Howard of Effingham* came to grief lying on its side at the bottom of an embankment at Shawford and, again, the driver and fireman scrambled out of the cab unhurt. At Shawford the up local and up through lines converge into one up line. The Nelson, with a Bournemouth–Waterloo train, was on the up local line. The junction points had been set, and the appropriate semaphore signal cleared, for an up boat train ex-Southampton Docks on the through line. The Nelson driver mistook the clear signal as applying to him, with the result that *Howard of Effingham* ran off the end of the local line, through a sand drag and pitched down the embankment. Fortunately, the coupling between the tender and the first coach parted and the train and passengers did not follow. Within minutes the passengers transferred themselves to the boat train, which had stopped alongside when its driver saw what had happened; within an hour or so the empty Bournemouth train had been hauled away, and the drama was over, except for the recovery of the Nelson. As it was out of reach of breakdown cranes, No 30854 was later jacked upright and winched up a temporary track laid at a slope of 1 in 13 on the side of the embankment. Ten days after the accident No 30854 was in Eastleigh Works, little the worse, and requiring only the removal of a few dents and a fresh coat of paint. In contrast, out of the 98 Southern diesel-electric locomotives which came along later, two were destined to be completely written off by accident damage.

SR Route Availability

	LN	N15	V
Victoria (Eastern) to Ramsgate via Herne Hill and Chatham	√	√	√
Victoria (Eastern) to Dover { via Chatham and Faversham / via Tonbridge and Ashford	√	√	√
Charing Cross and Cannon St to Chislehurst (prohibited, middle road and local lines, Charing Cross Bridge)	—	√	√
Tonbridge to Bopeep Jct	—	—	√
Swanley to Ashford	√	√	√
Ashford to Ore	—	—	√
Ashford to Minster Jct via Canterbury West	—	√	√
Folkestone Harbour branch	√	√	√
Dover to Ramsgate via Deal	√	√	√
Holborn Low Level and Holborn Viaduct to Herne Hill	—	—	—
North Kent East Jct to Charlton via Greenwich	—	—	√
Charlton to Maidstone West via Strood	√	√	√
Paddock Wood to Maidstone West	—	—	—
Victoria (Central) to East Croydon	√	√	√
London Bridge to Brighton via Redhill or Quarry	√	√	√
Three Bridges to Horsham	√	√	√
Keymer Jct to Eastbourne and Ore	√	√	√
Streatham South Jct to Arundel Jct via Dorking	—	—	—
Preston Park and Brighton to Havant	√	√	√
South Croydon to Hurst Green Jct and Tunbridge Wells Central	—	—	√
Hurst Green Jct to East Grinstead	—	—	—
Tonbridge, Redhill and Guildford	√	√	√
Waterloo and Reading	√	√	√

	LN	*N15*	*V*
Guildford and Reading via Blackwater or Frimley and Ascot	60	60	60
Waterloo to Weymouth, and Exeter St Davids	√	√	√
Waterloo to Portsmouth Harbour via Woking or Cobham	√	√	√
Exeter to Okehampton	—	40	—
Okehampton to Plymouth	—	—	—
Brookwood to Winchester via Alton	√	√	√
Eastleigh to Portsmouth via Botley	√	√	√
St Denys to Fareham (20 mph over Hamble Viaduct)	—	—	√
Basingstoke to Reading	√	√	√
Enborne Jct (Newbury) to Shawford Jct	—	—	—
Southampton to Salisbury via Nursling or Eastleigh	√	√	√
Romsey to Andover (from Kimbridge Jct)	—	—	—
Brockenhurst to Lymington Pier	—	—	—
Brockenhurst to West Moors	—	—	—
West Moors to Hamworthy Jct	√	√	√
Salisbury to West Moors (from Alderbury Jct)	—	—	√
Templecombe to Broadstone	—	50	50
Coleford Jct to Ilfracombe	—	—	—

√ = *permitted*; 40 = *speed limit 40mph*; — = *barred*.

Note: Route permission was given by the Civil Engineer on the basis of daily running. On some prohibited routes, occasional trips were permitted in emergency or for special trains.

SR Tender Locomotives
(circa 1938-9)

20,000lb Tractive Effort and over

Nelsons	4-6-0	16		U, UI	2-6-0	71
Arthurs	4-6-0	74		K	2-6-0	17
H15	4-6-0	26		Q	0-6-0	20
S15	4-6-0	45		700	0-6-0	30
T14*	4-6-0	10		H‡	4-4-2	11
N15X†	4-6-0	7		Schools	4-4-0	40
N, N1	2-6-0	86		D15	4-4-0	10

18,000lb Tractive Effort and over

C	0-6-0	108		L, L1	4-4-0	37
C2, C2X	0-6-0	48		S11	4-4-0	10
C3	0-6-0	8		K10, L11	4-4-0	80
E, E1	4-4-0	26		B4, B4X	4-4-0	13

Under 18,000lb Tractive Effort

O1	0-6-0	54		T6	4-4-0	1
O395	0-6-0	18		X6, T3	4-4-0	6
B1, F1	4-4-0	41		X2	4-4-0	1
D, D1	4-4-0	51				
L12	4-4-0	20		B4	4-4-0	7
T9	4-4-0	66		A12	0-4-2	13

*'Paddleboxes'; †'Remembrances'; ‡Atlantics.

Locomotive Summaries

KING ARTHURS
Urie N15 class (built Eastleigh Works)

SR No	New	Name	Withdrawn
736	8/18	Excalibur	11/56
737	10/18	King Uther	6/56
738	12/18	King Pellinore	3/58
739	2/19	King Leodegrance	5/57
740	3/19	Merlin	12/55
741	5/19	Joyous Gard	2/56
742	6/19	Camelot	2/57
743	7/19	Lyonesse	10/55
744	9/19	Maid of Astolat	1/56
745	11/19	Tintagel	2/56
746	6/22	Pendragon	10/55
747	7/22	Elaine	10/56
748	8/22	Vivien	9/57
749	9/22	Iseult	6/57
750	10/22	Morgan le Fay	7/57
751	11/22	Etarre	6/57
752	12/22	Linette	12/55
753	1/23	Melisande	3/57
754	2/23	The Green Knight	1/53
755	3/23	The Red Knight	5/57

Maunsell N15 class (built Eastleigh Works)

448	5/25	Sir Tristan	8/60
449	6/25	Sir Torre	12/59
450	6/25	Sir Kay	9/60
451	6/25	Sir Lamorak	6/62
452	7/25	Sir Meliagrance	8/59
453	2/25	King Arthur	7/61
454	3/25	Queen Guinevere	11/58

Maunsell N15 class (built North British Locomotive Co)

SR No	New	Name	Withdrawn
455	3/25	Sir Launcelot	4/59
456	4/25	Sir Galahad	5/60
457	4/25	Sir Bedivere	5/61
763	5/25	Sir Bots de Ganis	10/60
764	5/25	Sir Gawain	7/61
765	5/25	Sir Gareth	9/62
766	5/25	Sir Geraint	12/58
767	6/25	Sir Valence	6/59
768	6/25	Sir Balin	10/61
769	6/25	Sir Balan	2/60
770	6/25	Sir Prianius	11/62
771	6/25	Sir Sagramore	3/61
772	6/25	Sir Percivale	9/61
773	6/25	Sir Lavaine	2/62
774	6/25	Sir Gaheris	1/60
775	6/25	Sir Agravaine	2/60
776	6/25	Sir Galagars	1/59
777	6/25	Sir Lamiel	10/61*
778	6/25	Sir Pelleas	5/59
779	7/25	Sir Colgrevance	7/59
780	7/25	Sir Persant	7/59
781	7/25	Sir Aglorale	5/62
782	7/25	Sir Brian	9/62
783	8/25	Sir Gillimere	2/61
784	8/25	Sir Nerovens	10/59
785	8/25	Sir Mador de la Porte	10/59
786	8/25	Sir Lionel	8/59
787	9/25	Sir Menadeuke	2/59
788	9/25	Sir Urre of the Mount	2/62
789	9/25	Sir Guy	12/59
790	9/25	Sir Villiars	10/61
791	9/25	Sir Uwaine	5/60
792	10/25	Sir Hervis de Revel	2/59

*Preserved.

Maunsell N15 class with six-wheel tenders (built Eastleigh Works)

SR No	New	Name	Withdrawn
793	3/26	Sir Ontzlake	8/60
794	3/26	Sir Ector de Maris	8/62
795	4/26	Sir Dinadin	7/62
796	5/26	Sir Dodinas le Savage	2/62
797	6/26	Sir Blamor de Ganis	6/59
798	6/26	Sir Hectimere	6/62
799	7/26	Sir Ironside	2/61
800	9/26	Sir Meleaus de Lile	8/61
801	10/26	Sir Meliot de Logres	4/59
802	10/26	Sir Durmore	7/61
803	11/26	Sir Harry le Fise Lake	8/61
804	12/26	Sir Cador of Cornwall	2/62
805	1/27	Sir Constantine	11/59
806	1/27	Sir Galleron	4/61

LORD NELSON
Maunsell LN class (built Eastleigh Works)

SR No	New	Name	Withdrawn
850	8/26	Lord Nelson	8/62*
851	6/28	Sir Francis Drake	12/61
852	7/28	Sir Walter Raleigh	2/62
853	9/28	Sir Richard Grenville	3/62
854	10/28	Howard of Effingham	9/61
855	11/28	Robert Blake	8/61
856	11/28	Lord St Vincent	9/62
857	12/28	Lord Howe	9/62
858	1/29	Lord Duncan	8/61
859	3/29	Lord Hood	12/61
860	4/29	Lord Hawke	8/62
861	9/29	Lord Anson	10/62
862	10/29	Lord Collingwood	10/62
863	10/29	Lord Rodney	2/62
864	11/29	Sir Martin Frobisher	2/62
865	11/29	Sir John Hawkins	5/61

*Preserved.

SCHOOLS
Maunsell V class (built Eastleigh Works)

SR No	New	Name	Withdrawn
900	3/30	Eton	2/62
901	5/30	Winchester	12/62
902	6/30	Wellington	12/62
903	6/30	Charterhouse	12/62
904	7/30	Lancing	7/61
905	7/30	Tonbridge	12/61
906	8/30	Sherborne	12/62
907	8/30	Dulwich	9/61
908	9/30	Westminster	9/61
909	9/30	St Paul's	2/62
910	8/32	Merchant Taylors	11/61
911	8/32	Dover	12/62
912	9/32	Downside	12/62
913	9/32	Christ's Hospital	2/62
914	10/32	Eastbourne	7/61
915	5/33	Brighton	12/62
916	5/33	Whitgift	12/62
917	5/33	Ardingly	11/62
918	6/33	Hurstpierpoint	10/61
919	6/33	Harrow	1/61
920	10/33	Rugby	11/61
921	11/33	Shrewsbury	12/62
922	12/33	Marlborough	11/61
923	12/33	Bradfield	12/62
924	12/33	Haileybury	1/62
925	7/34	Cheltenham	12/62
926	7/34	Repton	12/62
927	7/34	Clifton	1/62
928	8/34	Stowe	11/62
929	8/34	Malvern	12/62
930	9/34	Radley	12/62
931	1/35	King's Wimbledon	9/61
932	2/35	Blundell's	1/61
933	3/35	King's Canterbury	11/61
934	4/35	St Lawrence	12/62
935	6/35	Sevenoaks	12/62

SCHOOLS

Maunsell V class (built Eastleigh Works)

SR No	New	Name	Withdrawn
936	7/35	Cranleigh	12/62
937	7/35	Epsom	12/62
938	8/35	St Olaves	7/61
939	8/35	Leatherhead	6/61

Bibliography

Berridge, P. S. A. *The Girder Bridge*. Robert Maxwell, 1969.

Bradley, D. L. *Locomotives of the London & South Western Railway*. Railway Correspondence and Travel Society.

Cocks, C. S. *History of Southern Railway Locomotives to 1938*. Inst. of Locomotive Engineers proceedings. Vol xxxviii, 1948.

Darwin, B. *War on the Line*. Southern Railway Co, 1946.

Dendy-Marshall, C. F. *The History of the Southern Railway*. Reprinted Ian Allan, 1968.

Holcroft, H. *Locomotive Adventure*. Ian Allan.

Kidner, R. W. *The Southern Railway*. Oakwood Press, 1958.

Moody, G. T. *Southern Electric 1909–1968*. Ian Allan, 1968.

Nock, O. S. *Southern Steam*. David & Charles, 1966.

Nock, O. S. *British Steam Locomotives at Work*. George Allen and Unwin, 1967.

E. S. Cox, W. A. Tuplin, John Powell, P. G. Johnson. *Royal Scots of the LMS*. Ian Allan, 1970.

Saklatvala, B. *Arthur: Roman Britain's Last Champion*. David & Charles, 1967.

White, H. P. *A Regional History of the Railways of Great Britain*. Vol II. David & Charles, 1961.